Praise for *On My Own Two Feet*

"*On My Own Two Feet* is a must-read for everyone. This book actually makes personal finance interesting. You will read it cover to cover. Go get a copy, and get copies for the people you care about. Taking care of your money is important, and the earlier you start, the better."

—Tim Westergren, founder, Pandora

"*On My Own Two Feet* is a must-read for all women who want to own their own destiny. In clear, penetrating prose, Thakor and Kedar guide their readers along the journey to financial security and personal freedom. Whether you are going to run a corporation, a household, or your own extraordinary life, this book is indispensable."

—Nancy F. Koehn, James E. Robison Professor of
Business Administration, Harvard Business School

"*On My Own Two Feet* is a uniquely helpful book for young women and men who seek true (financial—if you want to use this word) independence. And it is not bad as a refresher for those who think they are already there. This short book is comprehensive, entertaining, and well organized. It will come in handy for easy reference. Makes for a thoughtful and timely gift for anyone who has young friends."

—Jim Crownover, chairman, Board of Trustees, Rice University

"This is the path to true liberation: how to handle all those hard-earned dollars. Or make do with what you've got. And if I were a modern boy, I'd put on a wig and buy one as well. We all need this guidebook."

—Lynn Sherr, ABC news correspondent and author,
Outside the Box: A Memoir

Praise for *On My Own Two Feet*

"This book is essential reading for everyone, not just females. It is particularly appropriate for anyone starting a career, leaving a financially secure environment, or anyone who isn't familiar with personal finance and budgeting. But, it's even a great reminder for those that have been actively managing their own financial future for many years. It is very readable and very sensible. You won't be sorry you picked it off the bookstore (or online) shelf."

—Jim Hackett, former chairman and CEO of Anadarko Petroleum
Corporation, former chairman of Federal Reserve Bank of Dallas

"On My Own Two Feet is the financial equivalent of the basic black dress and red handbag in every woman's closet. Choose it early and use it often for maximum positive effects. I mentor many young women, and this book will be one of my recommended financial tools as they build for future professional and personal dreams."

—Betsy Heller Cohen, vice president and futurist,
Nestlé Purina PetCare Company

"A book on personal finance is probably not most women's first choice when they're looking for some captivating reading. However, *On My Own Two Feet* is that wonderful combination of practical information that can transform your life delivered in a clear, concise, and motivating tone. Whether you're just starting out in your career, brushing up on knowledge ahead of a financial decision, or trying to reorient your overall relationship with money, this is the book you need to guide you through."

—Caryn Effron, founder, GoGirl Finance

Praise for *On My Own Two Feet*

"*On My Own Two Feet* isn't just a must-read for women seeking financial empowerment. It's a book that women actually will read! Conversational and wise, practical and aspirational, this guide makes good on its promise to lead the reader to 'financial nirvana' with simplicity and style."

—Eleanor Blayney, CFP®, consumer advocate for CFP Board,
and author of *Women's Worth: Finding Your Financial Confidence*

"A financial how-to every woman should have on her bookshelf. *On My Own Two Feet* is clear, concise, and offers a wealth of knowledge that is unmatched in its ability to empower the reader, and set them off on the right track to become financially savvy and independent."

—Stacy Francis, founder, Savvy Ladies

"When I was putting together a class at the University of Michigan to teach undergraduates the research and practicalities about fostering lifelong health and physical well-being, I knew I'd be doing them a disservice if I didn't address their financial well-being. After searching for a user-friendly text on this topic for this broad class, I discovered *On My Own Two Feet*. It was the perfect text! My students routinely express gratitude for having had the opportunity to access this information through such a well-written and easy-to-grasp book. *On My Own Two Feet* is a must-read for anyone—high school students, college students, young professionals, or newly married couples, etc.—who needs an overview of the key steps to create a secure and healthy financial life."

—Michelle Segar, PhD, MPH, associate director,
Sport, Health, and Activity Research and Policy (SHARP)
Center for Women and Girls at the University of Michigan

Praise for *On My Own Two Feet*

"I'm crazy about this book. It is a must for every woman who wants to move more easily through life with a good, basic understanding of personal finance. It is a book that can help our grandmothers, mothers, daughters, and girlfriends get on top of their money issues quickly and confidently."

—Susan Harmon, former managing director, Public Radio Capital

"For over 130 years, Wellesley College has been creating 'cycles of empowerment,' experiences through which our students, having been empowered at the college, graduate and find ways to empower others around the world. The new book by Wellesley alumna Manisha Thakor and coauthor Sharon Kedar is a wonderful example of that process. Manisha and Sharon have discovered how much their own independence, autonomy, and freedom depends on their willingness to learn the essentials of money management. In *On My Own Two Feet* they communicate their hard-won knowledge so that others can experience the independence, autonomy, and freedom that women so deserve, and too often still lack. Every woman—of every age and circumstance—can benefit from this book. Knowledge is power."

—Diana Chapman Walsh, PhD, former president, Wellesley College

ON MY OWN

TWO FEET

2ND EDITION

a modern girl's guide to
personal finance

Save and Invest Wisely • Achieve Financial Security
Own Your Finances, Own Your Life

Manisha Thakor, MBA, CFA, and Sharon Kedar, MBA, CFA

Adams Media
New York London Toronto Sydney New Delhi

Adams Media
An Imprint of Simon & Schuster, Inc.
57 Littlefield Street
Avon, Massachusetts 02322

For information about special discounts for bulk purchases, please contact Simon & Schuster Special Sales at 1-866-506-1949 or business@simonandschuster.com.

The Simon & Schuster Speakers Bureau can bring authors to your live event. For more information or to book an event contact the Simon & Schuster Speakers Bureau at 1-866-248-3049 or visit our website at www.simonspeakers.com.

Manufactured in the United States of America

10 9 8 7

Library of Congress Cataloging-in-Publication Data has been applied for.

ISBN 978-1-4405-7084-1
ISBN 978-1-4405-7113-8 (ebook)

to all women

Contents

PART A

The Tools for Financial Empowerment...19

PART B

The Path from Saving to Investing...77

PART C

The Strategies for Real-Life Situations...121

APPENDICES

Foreword to the New Edition

Timeless financial advice. Does it really exist?

When the first edition of *On My Own Two Feet* came out in 2007, the world was a very different place. The stock market, the job market, and real estate markets were all strong. Economic optimism abounded.

While we never could have predicted that just a year after our first edition came out, our nation would experience the worst recession and stock market performance since the Great Depression, that's exactly what happened. Major financial institutions quite literally fell apart. In a highly controversial move, the U.S. government even stepped in to save those corporations it deemed too important to fail. Just a year after this book's initial publication, money stuffed under the mattress suddenly seemed the best path— not so far off the attitudes that prevailed in the 1930s following the Great Depression. Yet, in those difficult years after 2008, the advice in this book remained just as applicable, just as relevant, and just as important as it was in the strong economy.

History has a funny way of repeating itself. Slowly, as our country dug out of the recession and the stock market began to creep upward again, it became clear that there is, in fact, timeless financial advice. It includes the steps advocated in *On My Own Two Feet*, such as living within one's means, starting to save early, and using low-cost diversified investment offerings.

That said, a few things *have* shifted since we first wrote *On My Own Two Feet*, and thus this second edition contains the following updates:

- **Time has passed:** We've updated the statistics throughout the book.
- **Legislation has passed and/or been introduced:** The Credit Card Act of 2009 helped curtail some of the most egregious abuses around late and penalty fees as well as the marketing to college students. Additional legislation is working its way through the system around the use of credit scores in the job search process. Our discussions of these topics have been updated to reflect the current state of affairs.
- **Young Americans are struggling in unprecedented numbers with student loan debt:** Since the original publication of this book, the total amount of student loans outstanding eclipsed the amount of total credit card debt for the first time. Ever. We've added a new chapter to the book on the basics of student loan debt.

Importantly, while the statistics have been updated in this 2nd edition of *On My Own Two Feet*, the core advice in this book remains the same. Tested by one of the most brutal patches in recent economic times a mere one year after its initial release, we feel more strongly than ever that the advice in this book can help get you on solid financial footing.

Another reason for the 2nd edition of *On My Own Two Feet* is that these vital basic tenets of personal finance are still not reaching as many people as they should. Consider the current financial literacy landscape:

- **Americans still aren't saving enough:** After the financial crisis of 2008–2009, the nation's savings rate crept upward to 5.1 percent in 2010. But the improved habits didn't last. A full 30 percent of workers in a 2012 EBRI study reported that they had less than $1,000 in savings and investments.
- **Americans continue to avoid budgeting:** According to the 2012 Consumer Financial Literacy Survey, 56 percent of Americans admit they have absolutely no budget.
- **Americans are not prepared for retirement:** Nearly 75 percent of retirees have not saved enough and said they would save more if they could do it all over again. According to Financial Finesse, fewer than 40 percent of employees feel confident that their retirement investments are properly allocated.

Since *On My Own Two Feet* was published in 2007, we have given speeches about the power of "Saving, Investing, and Protecting Yourself" to thousands of women from coast to coast. After what seemed like every presentation, the same thing would happen: Woman after woman would come up to us and tell us that she wished she had heard this information sooner. Today, we're happy to say that enough time has gone by that we're starting to hear the opposite—early readers of *On My Own Two Feet* have contacted us to triumphantly exclaim, "I did it! I read your book, followed the steps, and wow, is my financial life the better for it."

So, if you are starting from (the very common place of) having no savings, a lot of credit card or student loan debt, or just feeling overwhelmed by the thought of investing, please know this: Time and again, we've seen how simply making a shift in your mindset to committing to improving your financial well-being can open a doorway to one of the most joyous of life journeys—to financial freedom.

Importantly, you don't have to love personal finance to take charge of this part of your life. Manisha truly does and Sharon does not. It doesn't matter, as long as you consistently act on the basics. Too many people miss that vital secret, thinking good personal finance habits require an advanced business degree and the ability to identify which company will be the next hot stock. This simply is not so. Please keep reading and go for it. Act on the basics. Own your finances, own your life.

Introduction

Have you been searching for a personal finance book that is short, inviting, and easy to read? If so, your search is over. *On My Own Two Feet* explains what you need to know about your money without drowning you in mind-numbing detail. This book will empower you to take charge of your financial life.

As graduates of Harvard Business School who have spent the majority of our careers working in the money management industry, we are frequently asked for suggestions on how people can best learn about personal finance. Time and again we hear the same lament, "I know I need to learn about this stuff, but it's just so boring and complex . . ."

▷ While a solid understanding of personal finance is important for both sexes, we are particularly concerned with helping women grasp the basic principles of money management.

By the time you are finished reading this book, you will know more about your money than the vast majority of Americans. You will be aware of the factors that drive your financial health, and you will understand how to routinely incorporate them into your daily life. For instance, in this book you will learn these key lessons:

- How to make your credit cards benefit you instead of the credit card companies

- How much of your income to save—not just for retirement, but also for near-term needs such as an emergency fund and key big-ticket items like a car and a home
- How to invest your savings so your money grows and lasts as long as you do

Today, many women are choosing to marry later in life or not at all. With divorce rates high, and given that women have statistically longer life spans than men, it is a basic fact of life that a high percentage of women will spend as much or more of their lives single than coupled. Therefore, it's unwise to think that Prince Charming is going to swoop in to solve your financial woes. In fact, it's probably safe to assume that Prince Charming doesn't have a clue when it comes to money, even if he acts like he does.

"Prince Charming" Is Not a Financial Plan

- Roughly 90 percent of American women will find themselves the sole keepers of their personal finances at some point during their lives, according to the National Center for Women and Retirement.
- According to the Transamerica Center for Retirement Studies, 28 percent of working women have taken or expect to take time out of the workforce to act as a caregiver for a child or aging parent. Of the women who plan to take time out of the workforce, 73 percent believe that it will negatively impact their ability to save for retirement and, ultimately, the size of their retirement nest egg.
- Two-thirds of women over age 65 rely on Social Security as their primary source of income. Consequently, women are twice as likely as men to live out their golden years at or below poverty levels, according to the National Women's Law Center and the Administration on Aging.

We are concerned that women continue to get shortchanged when it comes to financial matters. It is this concern that inspired us to write *On My Own Two Feet*. In light of these statistics, our personal goal is to help our fellow females. Nevertheless, the core of our financial advice is equally applicable to men.

Having worked in the financial services industry, we have seen firsthand the power of learning just a few simple financial lessons. These lessons are useful at any age. However, they are most powerful when implemented in your twenties and thirties because you have more time on your side. The sooner you implement the basics of personal finance, the more confidence and financial security you will have. You will also eliminate a major source of stress and fear later in life. Simply put, understanding how to balance your desire to live well today with the need to save and invest for tomorrow is the equivalent of reaching financial nirvana. Helping you achieve this vision is the goal of this book.

Money Madness

When it comes to money and personal finance, millions of people are caught up in a perfect storm. They want to believe that everything will work out okay.

However, they aren't quite sure what to do with their money or how it all adds up. To add insult to injury, in modern America we are bombarded with images encouraging us to buy more stuff. This relentless emphasis on materialism subtly teaches us to judge people not by who they *are* but by what they *have*. It is a value system that tempts us to live beyond our means.

For instance, if you see a woman dressed in designer jeans, stylish heels, and the latest trendy handbag, you might think, "Wow, she's arrived." However, the reality quite often is, "Dang, she's just one paycheck away from losing it all."

▷ The stark reality is that despite outward appearances of affluence, a shocking number of people are literally just a stone's throw away from financial disaster.

This is just as true for men as for women. The next time you see a guy cruise by in a shiny new sports car, keep in mind that you may very well be looking at his biggest asset. Unfortunately, all too many Americans are caught up in an unending cycle of spending more than they earn as they strive to maintain lifestyles that project images way beyond what they can afford.

Consider These Shocking Statistics

- According to the American Payroll Association, nearly 70 percent of Americans are living essentially paycheck to paycheck.
- In terms of their greatest financial priority right now, the majority of working women (55 percent) are focused on paying off debt, such as their credit cards, or just getting by—covering basic living expenses. For unmarried working women, this number jumps to 64 percent, according to the Transamerica Center for Retirement Research.
- Far fewer working women have a retirement strategy—just over half (52 percent) have a retirement strategy, only 11 percent of whom have a written plan, according to Transamerica.

It's not that people want to make bad financial decisions—it's that they never learned the basics. Personal finance is not taught in most schools, and talking about money is still taboo in many circles. Parents often assume children will pick up the basics of personal finance on their own, and many parents don't really have a grip on their own finances. As a result, millions of Americans simply do not know how to live within their means.

Author John Naisbitt has said, "We are drowning in information and starved for knowledge." This is particularly true in the realm of money. One of the fundamental premises of *On My Own Two Feet* is that the "right" personal finance guidance is already out in the public domain—it's just tough to identify it in the sea of available information.

▷ In this book, therefore, we home in on the most
   important aspects of personal finance and skip the
   extraneous details.

On My Own Two Feet is divided into three parts. In the first section, we will walk you through the five basic tools for financial success. In the second section, we'll discuss how to invest your hard-earned savings. In the final section, we'll address strategies for dealing with potentially tricky real-life situations, including those student loans you're probably carrying. Should you wish to delve deeper into any of these topics, we list a variety of resources in the appendices. The bottom line is that if you want to be in charge of your future, you need to have control over your finances. So let's get started.

PART A

THE TOOLS FOR FINANCIAL EMPOWERMENT

CHAPTER 1

Start Saving Now

The first step toward financial success is to develop the habit of saving. Developing this habit is a lot like developing the habit of flossing your teeth. It's hard to argue against either practice in theory. However, when it comes to actually doing it, well, that's where most people fall short. So in this chapter we're going to spark your enthusiasm for saving by doing the following:

- Explaining why it is so important to save regularly
- Talking about when to start saving
- Discussing how much to save

Our goal is for you to come away from this chapter with a strong desire to start saving right now.

Why Save?

At its core, saving is really about spending. The whole reason you save money today is so that you can spend it in the future. In general, you save for three basic reasons:

1. To have a cushion—or an emergency fund—when life's unexpected expenses arise

2. To be able to pay for big-ticket items in the future
3. To ensure a financially secure retirement

Let's talk about each of these three reasons to save in a little more detail.

EMERGENCY FUND

According to the National Bureau of Economic Research, 50 percent of Americans would struggle to come up with $2,000 in a pinch. A whopping 64 percent of Americans do not have enough savings on hand to handle even a $1,000 emergency expense, according to the National Foundation for Credit Counseling.

This lack of savings can put you in a real bind when those unexpected bills pop up. Suppose you are laid off, and it takes a few months to find a new job. In the interim, you'd still have to pay your bills. This is why it's important to save enough money to cover at least three to six months of living expenses. Once you have this cushion, you'll find it easier to navigate through life's short-term detours.

BIG-TICKET ITEMS

Then there are the classic big-ticket items that you may want down the road. Examples of such items include a car, graduate school, a down payment for a home, a wedding, or your children's education. The key to buying big-ticket items without incurring burdensome debt is to start saving for them well in advance.

RETIREMENT

If you are like most people under the age of 50, retirement is probably the last thing on your mind. This is totally understandable. It seems so far off, and besides, you have career ladders to climb, families to build, friendships to cultivate, and hobbies to pursue. Unfortunately, our generation doesn't have the luxury of pushing off retirement planning the way previous generations did. Why? Well, fifty years ago, people retired in their mid-sixties and expected to live for another ten or so years on average. They funded their retirement with what was called a "three-legged stool," which included a company-sponsored pension plan, Social Security, and modest personal savings.

These days, it's the rare company that provides the kind of pension plan our grandparents and/or some of our parents received. As for Social Security, there's no guarantee it will be around when you retire, and as of this writing the average female beneficiary gets less than $1,100 a month. That means you'll need to rely on your own savings. As if this isn't enough, unlike prior generations, you are likely to live much longer. If you are in your twenties or thirties right now, there's a good chance you could live well into your nineties. That means you could live in retirement for twenty or thirty years—or two to three times longer than your grandparents *and* nearly as many years as you worked. Think about that for a minute. For each year you work, you might have to fund not only a year of current living expenses but also potentially a year of living expenses in retirement. Therefore, in addition to building an emergency fund and saving for big-ticket items, you must develop a long-term plan for retirement.

When to Start Saving

With these goals in mind, let's talk about when to start saving.

▷ Start saving today.

Asking when to start saving is like asking your dermatologist when to start wearing sunscreen. The answer is always right now. The reason is that the *sooner* you start a disciplined program of saving, the *less* you will have to save out of your own pocket. Let's look at Tabitha and Tonya. Their experiences highlight why it is so important to start saving as soon as you can.

The Tale of Two Ts: Tabitha and Tonya

Tabitha saved $5,000 a year for her retirement. Tonya saved $10,000 a year. Both women saved these amounts for ten years, made the same investments, and saw their money grow at 7 percent per year. Guess who had more money at age 65? At first glance, it may appear to be Tonya, but it's actually Tabitha.

TABITHA'S STORY

Tabitha graduated from college and, at age 22, took a job working for an accounting firm in Dallas with a starting salary of $40,000. Right away, she began saving $5,000 a year for her retirement. Tabitha kept up this routine for ten years, *saving a total of $50,000 out of her own pocket*. Then, at age 32, she decided to quit her job to become a full-time mother. While she did not contribute another dollar to her savings, her existing nest egg continued to grow for thirty-three more years before she hit retirement age at 65.

TONYA'S STORY

Tonya, by contrast, graduated from college and took a job working for an ad agency in San Francisco with a starting salary of $30,000. In her early days, money was very tight. Living in the high-cost Bay Area, just making her rent was a struggle, so Tonya did not save anything in her younger years. A talented and creative individual, Tonya quickly moved up the ranks at the ad agency. By age 42, she was a vice president and was making $75,000 a year. Tonya finally felt like she was able to start saving for retirement, so she began putting away $10,000 a year. Tonya did this for ten years, *saving a total of $100,000 out of her own pocket.* At age 52, however, when her parents became very ill, she decided to quit her job to help take care of them and she stopped saving. Tonya's existing nest egg only got to grow for thirteen more years before she hit age 65.

THE MAGIC OF TIME

While both women's investments grew at 7 percent a year, their nest eggs at age 65 were very different sizes. When Tabitha turned 65, her retirement nest egg had blossomed into a whopping $644,000. When Tonya turned 65, her retirement nest egg had reached $333,000. While Tabitha saved only half as much as Tonya out of her own pocket, she ended up with nearly two times *more* than Tonya in her retirement nest egg. How did this happen? The reason is very simple. Tabitha started saving twenty years *earlier* than Tonya.

▷ Saving *early* gives your money more *time* to grow.

The benefits of starting to save and invest early are simply enormous. Having *time* on your side and investing your hard-earned savings in a smart manner is the classic recipe for financial success.

How Much to Save

We know how hard it is to save. We also recognize that many of you are just making ends meet. However, we'd be doing you a real disservice if we didn't give you the straight scoop when it comes to how much you need to save if you want to be financially secure. *Ideally, 15 percent of your gross income is the amount to save ("gross" income simply means your income before any taxes are taken out).* Recall that you save money for three future needs: emergencies, big-ticket items, and your retirement.

We recommend setting aside 5 percent of your gross income for your combined emergency fund and big-ticket items and 10 percent of your gross income for your retirement. Your main vehicle for your retirement savings will be your employer-sponsored retirement savings plan—such as your 401(k)—and your individual retirement account (IRA). **CHAPTER 9** discusses these important accounts.

It's very important to note that the precise breakdown of your savings may vary from year to year. For instance, if you do not yet have an emergency fund, you'll put more of your savings toward that goal first. Alternately, if you are trying to save for a down payment for a home, you'll put more of your savings toward that goal. The key point to take away is that while your percentage mix among these categories may vary over time . . .

▷ If you save at least 15 percent of your gross income year in and year out—and are careful about your investments—you'll be firmly on your way to financial nirvana.

Over time, you will build up enough cash to cover three to six months of living expenses in case you hit one of life's little rough patches. You will have the ability to make those big-ticket purchases without having to take on heavy levels of debt. Finally, you should be able to retire free from financial worry. Who wouldn't want all that?

You may be thinking, "Save 15 percent of my income, with at least two-thirds of that going toward my retirement—are you crazy? Heck, life's short. I'm saving to buy those hot new heels I saw in my favorite department store!" We agree that it's important to enjoy the present. However, ignoring your future while living it up today can lead to financial disaster later in life. It can also set you up for high stress during your working days. So go for it. Give yourself the gift of financial security by starting to save as early as you possibly can.

▷ Even if you save just a small percentage of your salary at first, the key is to know your end goal and start working toward reaching it.

If you want to see approximately what you'd end up with in your golden years if you start saving 10 percent of your gross income today for retirement, please see the chart in **APPENDIX A**.

Where Do I Store My Savings?

- **Day-to-day needs:** Store the money you need to access for your day-to-day needs in a checking account at your preferred bank or credit union. In **APPENDIX A**, we list some questions to help you find the one that's right for you.
- **Emergency fund and big-ticket items:** Store this money in a savings account at the same bank or credit union as your checking account or consider putting that savings in a money market fund at a diversified financial institution or brokerage house. These types of firms typically offer a wider range of investment products and services than traditional

banks and credit unions. We list contact information for several large, established diversified financial institutions in **APPENDIX A**.

- **Retirement savings:** There are two types of special accounts that you can use to super-size your retirement savings. These accounts are so important that we've devoted an entire chapter (**CHAPTER 9**) to explaining how they work.

As you strive to start, increase, or maintain your savings rate, a great approach is to put your savings on autopilot. You can make your financial life much easier by setting up automatic deposits. For instance, you can ask your employer to make automatic deposits into your retirement account. You can also have a portion of your paycheck deposited directly into your savings account at your bank or into your account at a discount brokerage firm. Setting up your savings on an automated monthly basis ensures it gets done.

Despite economic ups and downs since the start of this century, the average American still saves practically nothing. To state the obvious, if you do not save money on a regular basis, you will not have a safety net when you hit life's inevitable potholes. Additionally, when it comes time for those big-ticket items that most people hope to buy, you must have savings to avoid taking on burdensome levels of debt. Finally, in order to have a comfortable retirement, saving is even more important for women than men given that women tend to live longer than men. To help you reach your savings goals, the next four chapters of this book are dedicated to the key tools you can use to find the money to save and achieve financial success. ■

Savings Tips When Money Is Tight

Starting is the first priority.

Remember, even if you can only save 3 percent or 5 percent of your gross income at first, know that every little bit counts and the money you save early on is the most valuable.

Knowledge is power.

Just understanding the importance of saving is a *huge* first step. If you make saving a priority, you will figure out how to increase your savings percentage over time.

Don't despair.

If you are reading this, and like many, many people are sitting there with piles of student loans or other debt, keep reading. By the time you finish this book, you'll have a solid roadmap for prioritizing debt pay-down and setting money aside for savings.

CHAPTER 2

Use Your Credit Cards Wisely

The second stop on your journey to financial success is a discussion about the proper management of your credit cards. Credit cards can be very helpful if they are used primarily to keep you from having to carry a lot of cash in your wallet. Too many people, however, mistakenly consider their credit card the ultimate sidekick with which to indulge the here and now: "So simple to use, and it never lets me down!" This kind of attitude can easily lead to excessive credit card debt. Unfortunately, what many people don't realize until *after* they've racked up a hefty balance is that credit card debt can be ferociously expensive. Uncontrolled credit card debt curtails your freedom to create the life that's right for you.

▷ Make no mistake, credit card debt can be as addictive and debilitating as getting hooked on drugs.

We've just been very blunt about our unfavorable viewpoint on credit card debt. That said, we fully recognize that there are many people whose credit card debt has resulted from simply trying to make ends meet—not from a desire to spend recklessly. Whatever your situation, the goal of this chapter is to inspire you to *stop* using your credit cards to incur debt unless it truly is a *real* emergency. The ideal way to use your credit card is to only charge items that you can afford to pay for in full when your monthly credit card bill arrives.

If you already have credit card debt, please be sure to pay close attention to **CHAPTER 10**, where we provide a straightforward game plan for prioritizing the repayment of your existing credit card debt.

Now, here's the good news: You don't need an MBA to manage your credit cards effectively. Being informed, attentive, and a little disciplined will take you a long way. In the pages ahead, you will learn the stark reality of just how much credit card debt really costs. You'll also learn about the common credit card pitfalls and how to avoid them. Armed with this knowledge, you'll be on your way to managing your credit cards effectively and one step closer to achieving financial success.

The True Cost of Credit Card Debt

Let's take a look at Elizabeth, who was getting an ulcer from thinking about her $5,000 in credit card debt. Elizabeth has a fairly typical card, with an 18 percent annual interest rate and a minimum monthly payment of 3 percent of the current outstanding balance on the card. She decided to bite the bullet, stop charging anything else on her card, and pay down her debt. Her initial plan was to pay just the minimum required payment each month. Elizabeth was feeling very proud of this game plan ("Hey, at least I'm not ignoring the bill.").

The following table shows what Elizabeth's credit card debt paydown would look like if she paid just the minimum balance due each month:

	Debt at Beginning of the Year	**Total of Minimum Required Monthly Payments**	Portion Applied to Cover "Interest Charges" **(This Is the Fee the Credit Card Company Charged Elizabeth to Borrow Money)**	Portion Applied to Reducing Debt	Debt at End of the Year
Year 1	$5,000	$1,679	$827	$852	$4,148
Year 2	$4,148	$1,393	$686	$707	$3,441
Year 3	$3,441	$1,156	$569	$587	$2,854
Year 4	$2,854	$959	$472	$487	$2,268
Year 5	$2,268	$795	$392	$403	$1,964
		↓	↓	↓	↓
Totals in . . . Year 34		**$9,850**	**$4,850**	**$5,000**	**$0**

Just paying the minimum required monthly payment means Elizabeth would wind up forking over a total of $9,850—almost *double* the amount of her $5,000 credit card debt. To add insult to injury, it would take her a whopping thirty-four years to pay it off.

What Elizabeth did not realize was that not all of her minimum required monthly payment would go toward reducing her debt. Trying to pay off your debt by making just the minimum monthly payments is a bit like trying to lose weight by dieting strictly all day long and then eating five glazed doughnuts right before going to bed. It's hard to make forward progress. With credit cards, what holds you back is the portion of that minimum monthly payment that goes to the credit card company for the interest charge. It's the amount shown in the shaded column in the chart, and it adds up to a big chunk of change. That interest is essentially the fee that the credit card company charges you in exchange for letting you borrow

money from them. The money from your monthly payment go
first to paying off your interest, and only *then* does the remaining
amount go toward paying down your original debt.

▷ What this meant for Elizabeth was that she'd be paying off her purchases well past the time they found
  their way into the city dump.

So the next time you think about putting a $150 pair of trendy
designer jeans on your credit card and only paying your minimum
required monthly payment, remember that those jeans could end up
costing you not $150 but $300. Just paying the minimum required
monthly amount could nearly double the cost of anything you purchase. Understanding the true cost of credit card debt will help you
decide whether that additional purchase is really worth it to you.

▷ A financially savvy woman knows: Credit cards are
  not free money.

By the way, if Elizabeth paid just $50 more per month, *every*
month, over her required minimum payment, she'd have all her
debt paid down in less than five years and reduce her total interest
payments to $1,950. That's still a lot, but it's not the whopping
$4,850 she'd pay in interest charges if she only made her minimum
required monthly payment.

If you are interested in calculating the figures for your specific situation, you can visit a website such as *www.bankrate.com* or *http://credit*
.about.com and use the credit card calculators (or go to a search engine
like Google, Yahoo, or Bing and type in "best credit card debt payoff
calculators" to find other sites). Enter your current outstanding balance, your interest rate, and either your minimum required payment

34

n amount you can afford to pay each month, and the
:ell you how long it will take to pay off your debt.
w the interest rate you are paying, look at your last
..wit card bill. If you don't have an old bill, call the phone number
on the back of your credit card and ask the representative for your
current interest rate. We highly recommend you do this.

Common Credit Card Pitfalls

The next step toward taking charge of your credit cards is to know
the traps and how to avoid them. These are the classic pitfalls:

1. Having too many credit cards
2. Thinking your interest rate is set in stone
3. Using your credit card to get cash from an ATM, or using
   those free checks that come in the mail
4. Falling victim to the new card "bait and switch"—you think
   you're getting a card with a low rate, but the card that actually arrives in the mail has a much higher rate
5. Being overly trusting

Let's talk about each of these traps and how to avoid them.

CLASSIC TRAP #1

TOO MANY CREDIT CARDS

We like to call having too many credit cards the credit card collection, or 3C, syndrome. Yes, this includes both traditional credit cards as
well as retail store cards! The problem with the 3C syndrome is twofold.

First, with too many cards, you may end up spending more in total than you realize. Second, with so many bills coming in, you increase the odds of not paying one of them on time. Paying late will hurt your financial reputation, trigger onerous late fees, and potentially result in higher penalty interest rates. Just like eating chocolate, when it comes to the number of credit cards to have, moderation is best.

> We recommend that you keep only two cards for personal use: one for regular use and a second to use as a backup only in emergencies. (If you have work-related expenses that are reimbursed by your employer, we think it's reasonable to have a third card dedicated exclusively to those purchases to help keep your reimbursement process simple.)

If you have too many credit cards today, know that you are not alone. Here's your action plan to whittle down that stack of plastic:

- If you are able to always pay off your entire balance at the end of each month, keep the two cards (or at most three, if you need one for work expenses) that are no-fee and/or have the best perks.
- If you're going to carry a balance on your cards (even for a few months), forget about perks. You need to identify your two existing cards with the lowest interest rates.
- Get out the scissors and slice up your remaining cards—just like you did those pictures of your ex-boyfriend. You're cutting up your cards to keep from charging more on them. However, until you pay off your entire balance(s) and officially close the account(s), you *must* continue to make your monthly payments.
- Once you have a zero balance on those extra cards, it's time to officially close them down. NOTE: As weird as it may sound,

timing matters when closing down these accounts. Please refer to **CHAPTER 3** and the discussion on credit scores before actually taking this step.

As for retail store cards, frankly, we're just not fans. They typically have *very* high interest rates. Additionally, as you'll learn in the next chapter, applying for these cards can hurt your financial reputation. While it may be tempting to open one to get that "10 percent discount on your next purchase," we urge you to take a pass. We think the potential downside more than offsets that one-time price break. There's a reason that retailers want you to open one of their store cards, and it's not to make life easier for you. If, for personal reasons, you feel strongly that you want to have a particular store card, then be sure to routinely pay off your bill each month on time and in full.

What You Need to Know about Credit Card "Perks"

- You often have to pay an annual fee to get perks (like frequent flyer miles or cash back) so you want to make sure the perks are worth it.
- Paying a fee for a card that offers frequent flyer miles is only worth it if you charge at least $8,000 a year, or about $650 a month. At that rate, you'll earn one airline ticket roughly every three years.
- Paying a fee for a card that offers cash back is only worth it if you get more cash back than what you pay for the card. For example, a card with a $60 annual fee that offers 1.5 percent cash back means you need to charge more than $4,000 a year ($60 ÷ 0.015), or about $325 a month, for the card to make economic sense.
- Don't buy things with your credit cards that you don't really need just to get the perk. If you do the math, you'll find out it's almost always cheaper to buy the perk outright.

CLASSIC TRAP #2

INTEREST RATES THAT CHANGE

The interest rate on a credit card doesn't always stay at its initial level. There are several ways that credit card companies can legally raise your rates. Your action plan is to be aware of these and watch out for them in the day-to-day use of your cards. Here's a list of the most common reasons for rate hikes:

● **Your 0 percent teaser rate expires:** There is a reason they are called "teaser" rates. If you have a low teaser rate, call the toll-free number on the back of your credit card and find out when that rate expires because your new interest rate will likely skyrocket. Ideally, you should pay off or transfer your balance before then. Sorry, but continually transferring your balance from one 0 percent card to another is not a smart long-term strategy as it does not address your underlying problem of having too much debt. The smart strategy is to work hard to pay off all your credit card debt. Also know that teaser rates on balance transfers often apply *only* to the trans-ferred balance—new charges made on that card could have a *much* higher rate and get paid off last. Always ask about this.

● **You are late in paying your credit card bill:** Let's say you put your credit card bill in the mail two days before it's due. Unfortunately, the mail is slow that month, and it takes three days to get to the credit card company. Not only will you be charged a late fee, but it's quite possible your interest rate could go up. It's not uncommon for a low introductory teaser rate of 0 percent to jump to a penalty rate over 20 percent just because your payment was late. So please, don't ignore the bill—even if that means opening it while drinking a glass of wine or eating a bowl of ice cream to dull the pain.

● **"Just because," with advance written notice:** It's a painful reality but true—a credit card company can change your rate with just forty-five days' written notice. It's right there in that small print they sent you with your original card.

CLASSIC TRAP #3
CASH ADVANCES AND "FREE" CHECKS

Credit cards typically have one interest rate for goods and services that you purchase with your card and then a *much* higher rate for cash advances and those "free" checks that periodically arrive in the mail. Additionally, the interest on cash advances and free checks frequently starts accruing the minute you use them. The bottom line is that you should not use your cards for either of these "conveniences" unless it's a *real* emergency. As with retail store cards, there is a reason why credit card companies send you free checks. Once again, it's not for your convenience.

CLASSIC TRAP #4
THE NEW CARD "BAIT-AND-SWITCH"

You may have signed up for a new card with a low interest rate, and yet the card that actually comes in the mail from the credit card company turns out to be at a much higher rate. Believe it or not, credit card companies can legally do this. The reason is that in the fine print, these offerings often state that the low rate is only for people who "qualify." *Always* check the actual interest rate on your new card after you get it in the mail.

CLASSIC TRAP #5

MISPLACED TRUST

It's sad but true. The world is filled with folks hoping to make a quick buck off unsuspecting individuals. The following list contains a few basic precautions you can take to protect yourself from unwanted intruders:

- If you receive any e-mails or phone calls from a credit card company, *do not respond or give any information.* This could very well be a hoax. Call your credit card company back using the phone number on your card to validate that it's an authentic e-mail or call. The credit card company will not be offended by your doing this.
- Credit card companies will often try to sell you a bunch of add-on services, such as credit card disability insurance and antitheft account monitoring. You don't need any of these add-ons.
- Tear up all unsolicited credit card offers or "free checks" that you get in the mail. Don't just throw them away intact because thieves can fish through your trash and attempt to sign up for the cards or use the checks under your name.
- If your card gets lost or stolen, report it immediately. You're only liable for $50 if you report a missing card within two business days of discovery.

Keep a photocopy of the fronts and backs of all your cards at home in a safe place. That way if your wallet gets lost or stolen, you know what was in there and whom to call to cancel your cards.

If we've done our job right in this chapter, you, not the credit card companies, will have the power over your credit cards. Importantly, you'll also avoid becoming part of the scary but true statistics when it comes to credit cards. Here are just two of them:

- Only 35 percent of Americans pay off their credit card balances in full each month, according to *www.bankrate.com*.
- This means the remaining 65 percent are being subject to interest rate charges on their balances. As of this writing, that average interest rate is 13 percent for fixed rate cards and 15 percent for variable rate cards.

Remember, charging things to your credit card that you can't pay off in full at the end of the month is going to cost you big time. Paying only your minimum monthly payment can easily double the cost of anything you purchase. ■

Maximize the Benefits of Credit Cards

Get rid of the excess plastic in your wallet.

Whittle your stack of credit cards down to three or fewer.

Spend some quality time with your cards.

Find out your interest rate, the penalty charges for late payments (both late fees and penalty interest rates), your credit limit, what happens if you charge more than that limit, and the annual fee on your card.

Pay your bill at least one week before the due date.

If you tend to forget things, put a "recurring appointment" on your calendar and/or use online bill pay. Most important, if you can possibly pay more than the minimum required monthly payment, by all means do so.

CHAPTER 3

Understand Credit Scores

The next tool to be aware of in your quest for financial success is one that, while often ignored or misunderstood, has a surprisingly wide reach.

Your car. Your house. Your cell phone. Your insurance. And possibly even . . . Your job.

What do these things all have in common? The answer may surprise you. The commonality is a three-digit number called your credit score. This three-digit number can dramatically impact your ability to obtain these items.

Your credit score is a number that summarizes how financially responsible you are deemed to be. It is based on a variety of factors, such as how conscientious you've been about paying your bills on time and how much debt you currently have outstanding relative to your credit limits. If you've never heard of a credit score, don't worry. By the time you are finished reading this chapter, you will have a solid understanding of this all-important financial metric. Specifically, you will learn the following:

- How your credit score influences your life
- How to find your personal credit score
- What your score is based on and how you can maintain or improve it

How Your Credit Score Influences Your Life

Your credit score is essentially your financial reputation in numeric form. One of the key reasons you should care about your credit score is that it is used by all kinds of organizations to decide if they want to loan money to you and, if so, how much and at what interest rate.

For instance, suppose you want to buy a house, and you need a home loan for $200,000. The first thing the lender is going to do is a little research to decide how creditworthy you are. If you have a good credit score, the lender will label you "highly creditworthy" and charge you a lower rate of interest on your loan. If you have a poor credit score, the lender will charge you a higher rate of interest on your loan. If you have a *really* poor credit score, the lender may refuse you a loan altogether.

Take the examples of Karyn and Katie. They each are buying their first home and need to borrow $200,000 for a mortgage. Karyn is a financially informed woman. She uses her credit cards wisely and follows the steps outlined in this book. As a result, Karyn has a really good credit score, and the lender charges her 5.0 percent interest on her mortgage.

Katie, by contrast, frequently pays her bills late and sometimes just ignores them altogether. Consequently, Katie has a poor credit score. The lender charges Katie 8.0 percent interest on her mortgage. You may be thinking, "So Katie's interest rate may be a little higher than Karyn's—what's the big deal?"

Well, take a look at the numbers. Katie's poor credit score means she pays $394 *more* per month than Karyn will for her mortgage payment (see the following table).

Karyn vs. Katie: The Cost of a $200,000 Mortgage Loan*

	Karyn's experience with her good credit score	Katie's experience with her poor credit score
Annual mortgage interest rate	5.0%	8.0%
Monthly mortgage payment	$1,074	$1,468
Total interest paid over the life of the mortgage	$186,500	$328,300

*Based on a thirty-year fixed-rate mortgage. See **CHAPTER 12** for more on mortgages.

As you can see, a poor credit score is going to cost you big time. Unfortunately, we're not just talking about the interest rate for your house or car loan. In some specific situations, a prospective employer may also ask your permission to run a credit check on you as part of their interview process. The logic here being if you have not been responsible with your money, you may not be an appropriate candidate for that position—particularly if it is a job involving financial matters. While legislation has been introduced—and in some states passed—to curb this practice, it's important to know this kind of background search may occur. Thus, your credit score could influence your ability to get hired for that dream job. It doesn't stop there. Even your insurance premiums could be higher if you have a poor credit score, or you could be denied coverage altogether. The good news is that your credit score is a fluid number that you can improve by following a few basic, commonsense steps. We'll talk about those steps in the last section of this chapter. First, however, let's talk about your personal credit score.

What Is Your Personal Credit Score?

You know your home phone number, your cell phone number, your Social Security number, and so on. However, unless you've recently applied for a mortgage or car loan, chances are your credit score is not on the tip of your tongue. It's time to change that. Finding out your credit score is an important step toward financial empowerment. If you have a good credit score, this chapter will teach you how to keep it that way. If you have a poor credit score, our goal is to inspire you to work to improve it and to provide a roadmap for how you can do that.

So how do you find out your personal credit score?

Well, before we get to that, we need to clarify something. You don't have just one credit score. You actually have three main credit scores. They are called FICO scores, named after the Fair Isaac Corporation (the company that created this scoring methodology).

Credit scores are calculated by credit bureaus. There are three major credit bureaus: Equifax, Experian, and TransUnion. Each one maintains its own file (called a credit report) on you. Credit bureaus get their data from a variety of sources. For instance, when you apply for a credit card, car loan, or a home mortgage, the entity from which you sought that loan reports it to the credit bureaus.

Unfortunately, not every credit bureau gathers the same information. This means each credit bureau may have different "credit data" on you. Additionally, each credit bureau places a slightly different weight on the data. As a result, each credit bureau potentially calculates a slightly different credit score for you. The credit bureaus do not release their exact formulas for calculating credit scores, so there is a bit of a black-box element to this whole process.

▷ The easiest way to find your personal credit score
  is to go to *www.myfico.com.*

On this website, you will pay approximately $40 (as of this writing), and in return you will get your FICO credit scores as calculated by two of the three big credit bureaus. If funds are tight an alternative is to just check one score. This will give you a rough sense of your financial reputation and cost you less money. Make sure, however, to get your FICO score, not a lower-priced alternative score. Your FICO score is the number most lenders will use. Also be careful of offers for "free credit scores" or "$1 credit scores" as in the fine print, you will typically see that in purchasing these you have signed up for some type of ongoing monitoring for which you pay a monthly fee.

FICO credit scores range from 300 to 850, with higher being better. Generally scores above 750 are considered to be very good; scores below 650 are considered poor; and scores below 600 are considered *really* poor. If you are between 650 and 750, you are in "reasonable" territory.

If you already know that you have a pretty good score, you don't need to recheck your credit *score*. However, as you'll soon learn, it's important to check your credit *reports* on an annual basis.

Credit Score Basics

Now let's talk about what your credit score is based on and how to maintain or improve it.

There are five primary elements upon which your FICO credit score is based:

- How conscientious you are about paying your bills on time
- Length of your credit history
- How much debt you have outstanding relative to your credit limits
- Number of loans or credit cards you've recently applied for
- Kinds of debt you've used in the past (mortgages, credit cards, car loans, etc.)

There are a few basic steps you can take to maintain or improve your credit score.

STEP #1

MAKE SURE YOUR CREDIT REPORTS ARE ACCURATE

Your credit score is derived from information stored on your credit reports. Your credit report is a file containing the details of your historical financial behavior (kind of like the files your doctor keeps on your health).

Unfortunately, credit reports can have mistakes in them. A study by the Federal Trade Commission indicated 5 percent of credit reports can have mistakes in them big enough to meaningfully impact your credit score; nearly a quarter of reports in the study had some form of lesser error. Given this, we recommend you check your credit reports once a year to make sure they are error free.

When you review your reports, be sure to look for the following:

- **Any personal information that isn't yours:** This would include a name that isn't yours, an errant Social Security number, or an address where you have not lived.

- **Any accounts that aren't yours:** This may be related to a mix-up with someone else's file or to an incident of identity theft. You'll want to be sure to check this carefully.
- **Any outdated information:** You'll want to look for any mention of "unpaid balances" that you have since paid off and any late payments that happened more than seven years ago (as these can be purged from your report).
- **Any incorrect information:** This could include incorrect notations for closed accounts, delinquencies you remedied but are not yet reported as such, more than one delinquent date, information from an ex-spouse, etc.

Inaccuracies on credit reports are such a big deal that the U.S. government has passed a law enabling each American to request a free copy of his or her credit reports from the big three credit bureaus annually to protect themselves. (Now, this is free access to your credit *reports*—not your resulting credit *score*.)

> You can request a *free* copy of your credit reports once a year from each of the three big credit bureaus by going to *www.annualcreditreport.com* or by calling 877-322-8228. A great way to maintain a year-round watch on your credit is to request one report every four months. Rotate which bureau you request from each time. **We *strongly* suggest that you start doing this right now.**

Here's one note of caution: Many "imposter" websites have sprung up that try to charge you to get your credit report. These imposter sites typically have names similar to the legitimate website, so it's important to remember that *www.annualcreditreport.com*

is the *only* website authorized by the U.S. government to provide free annual credit reports.

STEP #2
ALWAYS PRACTICE GOOD FINANCIAL HOUSEKEEPING

The simplest way to keep a good credit score or improve a poor one is to *always* pay *all* of your bills on time. So, yes, this means opening up your bills even when what you really want to do is to just stick them under a big pile of stuff and deal with them later. It's not fun to have to pay bills. We won't try to convince you otherwise. If you've ignored bills in the past, you're not alone.

STEP #3
TAKE THESE EXTRA ACTIONS

Follow these additional tips if you are working to maintain or improve your credit score:

- **Keep the amount that you owe on your credit cards as low as possible.** Remember that your credit score is negatively impacted by how much debt you have outstanding relative to your credit limits. This is called your "debt utilization ratio." Paying down your credit card debt and keeping it as low as possible will reduce your debt utilization ratio and help your credit score.
- **Try to keep your oldest credit card account open.** Keeping this account open makes your credit history longer and helps your score. However, if you are being charged an annual fee on this card, rarely use this card, and already have a good credit score, go ahead and close the account.

- **Don't close down other old credit card accounts if you are within eighteen months of making a major purchase (such as a car or home).** As weird as this may sound, closing down your older credit card accounts can actually hurt your credit score as it shortens the length of your credit history.
- **If you are shopping for a car or home loan, keep it to a two-week period.** Creditors get nervous when they see you applying for a lot of credit. However, they also recognize that you may shop around for a car or home loan. If you keep your car or home loan shopping to a two-week period or less, these related credit inquiries will all be lumped together and count as only one request.
- **Don't apply for a bunch of credit cards all at once.** As we just mentioned, creditors get nervous when they see you applying for a bunch of new loans or additional credit cards. This is where those retail store cards can really get you into trouble. If you have so-so credit, it's not a good idea to apply for a new credit card just to save 10 percent on a sweater you like.

As you work either to maintain or improve your credit score, remember that you are taking a very important step toward achieving financial success. Your ability to access key things you may want in life such as a car, a home, or even potentially that dream job will increase as you improve your credit score. So stay on it—make sure your credit reports are accurate and that you are taking all the possible steps to maximize your credit score. ■

Maximize Your Financial Reputation

A high credit score is a goal well worth striving for.

Your credit score has a huge impact on your financial life, including what you pay for your home loan, car loan, and insurance.

Know your credit score.

If you don't know it, we recommend going to *www.myfico.com* and spending the money to check it. This will enable you to see your starting point.

Check your credit reports at least once a year.

We recommend setting a recurring appointment on your calendar. Remember, you can get access to your credit reports *free* (now, that's your credit *reports*, not your credit *score*) once a year at *www .annualcreditreport.com*, or by calling 877-322-8228.

CHAPTER 4

Protect Yourself with Insurance

If you're like most people, the mere sound of the word "insurance" is enough to make your eyes glaze over. This response is quite understandable. Most people don't like to focus on what can go wrong. It's much more fun to think about what's going right in your life. That said, insurance is pretty darn important for protecting your financial well-being. In this chapter, you will learn about:

- Three types of insurance you must have
- Three other types of insurance you need to know about
- Suggestions for purchasing insurance

It is important to understand that you are paying your "premium" (the cost of your insurance plan) hoping that you will never have to collect on the benefit offered by the insurance company. We realize it's a bit counterintuitive to tell you to buy something you hope to never have to use, but keep reading and you'll see why insurance is absolutely essential.

▷ The way we recommend you think about insurance
  is that you are buying something intangible but
  extremely precious. You are buying peace of mind.

Three Critical Types of Insurance

There are three kinds of insurance that everyone should have.

HEALTH INSURANCE

We're starting with health, because that's the most important. If you have to cut back elsewhere to afford health insurance, please do so. Your health is extremely precious. It's worth protecting.

Unfortunately, all too many people do go without health insurance. According to the U.S. government data, more than 27 percent of young adults did not have health insurance as of 2011. This is concerning because, as we all know, you don't get advance notice before you break a bone or, worse, find yourself afflicted with a serious illness. Health insurance provides you with the peace of mind to know that while medical expenses can be very costly, if something really awful happens, you will only have to pay a portion of the costs and your insurance company will help pay for the rest. Jasmine's story helps illustrate why health insurance is so important.

Jasmine just quit her job. She simply couldn't stand another day working for her former boss. Jasmine didn't have much in savings, so she decided to go without health insurance until she found another job. She figured she'd be fine. After all, she didn't smoke and was in great shape. Running late for a celebratory evening out with her friends, she tripped and fell as she ran down a steep flight of stairs, breaking her hand in three places. The fractures were severe and required surgery. The total out-of-pocket cost to Jasmine—who had no health insurance—was over $10,000. Ouch, indeed.

The key with health insurance is to get it. On top of helping you pay for medical bills, insurance companies also act as "negotiators" to get doctors and hospitals to lower their costs. Without insurance, not only will the expenses come out of your own pocket, but you'll also end up paying higher prices.

If you work for a company (or are a student at a college or university) that offers health insurance, that is generally the most convenient and cost-effective place to get your insurance. If you are married and both you and your spouse have health care through your employers (or schools), evaluate the policies offered by both organizations to decide which plan is best for each of you. Health insurance can be very complicated, so don't be afraid to ask questions in order to fully understand your options and their costs. (Note: As of this writing, federal legislation regarding health care is still being sorted out. The establishment of health-care exchanges may improve access to health insurance in the future for Americans of all ages. For the latest information, visit *www.healthcare.gov.*)

While there are many types of health-care plans, the two most common are health maintenance organizations (HMOs) and preferred provider organizations (PPOs). An HMO is typically lower in cost but has less flexibility. You are only allowed to see doctors that work for your HMO and usually must start any treatment by first visiting your general practitioner (your "gatekeeper"). With a PPO, you can typically see any doctor listed in your plan network whenever you want. In return for that flexibility, however, you'll usually pay higher premiums than you would with an HMO. It's ultimately a personal choice whether you want to pay more for the flexibility of a PPO.

If you don't have access to health insurance through work or school, you will need to buy coverage on your own by contacting a health insurer or insurance broker directly. If money is tight and you're stretching to buy any health insurance, we suggest you purchase a low-cost, high-deductible, catastrophic plan. (A deductible is the amount you have to pay out of your own pocket before your insurance kicks in.) A catastrophic plan will not cover routine doctor visits or prescription drugs, but it will provide coverage if something major goes wrong.

Unfortunately for Jasmine, she didn't realize that if you are leaving your company or are laid off, you have sixty days to apply for an extension of your health-care coverage offered by your employer, under a plan called COBRA. This applies to companies with twenty or more employees, and offers coverage of up to eighteen months under most circumstances. You'll need to pay your entire premium (that is, your employer won't be paying for a portion of your monthly premiums as they would if you were still employed), but it's generally a straightforward way to keep health-care coverage while you are between jobs. It also enables you to avoid the hassle of having to be screened for pre-existing conditions the way you would if you signed up with a new insurance company on your own. You are legally entitled to coverage under COBRA, so checking into this should be one of the first things you do when you prepare to leave a job.

If you have a little extra financial wiggle room, you can upgrade to a more comprehensive policy that covers preventive doctor visits and prescription drugs. Depending on the type of plan you select, your health, your age, and any pre-existing conditions, premiums can begin around $100 per month and go to more than $500 per month. In the last section of this chapter, we provide some suggestions for purchasing insurance.

AUTO INSURANCE

In our hurried, on-the-go society, car accidents happen. As a result, most states have mandatory minimum amounts of auto insurance that you must purchase to legally own a car, truck, or motorcycle. An auto insurance policy has two parts. The first part that we'll discuss (because we think it's the most important) is called liability coverage.

Auto Insurance Part 1: Liability Coverage

If you are responsible for an accident, liability coverage is the portion of your auto insurance that will provide financial protection to you for the damage that you cause to others—to both their bodies and their cars.

▷ Liability is the part of an auto accident that can really mess up your finances.

Without enough liability coverage, if you are found at fault for causing an accident, you may have to pay someone not just out of your current savings but also potentially from your future earnings.

Jenny had an allergy-induced sneezing fit and her car drifted across the median and hit another car head on. Both the driver and the front passenger suffered serious injuries and were out of work for months. Thankfully, Jenny had adequate liability coverage. The folks she hit hired a personal injury lawyer who went after Jenny like a hungry tiger for their lost wages, medical expenses, and car damage as well as compensation for their pain and suffering due to Jenny's carelessness in driving. Since Jenny had purchased an auto policy with liability coverage limits that exceeded the legal fees and settlement amount, she merely owed her deductible.

You want to be extra sure not to scrimp on your liability coverage. Liability coverage has three parts. The price you pay for this portion of your auto insurance depends on how much coverage you select for each of the following:

1. For each person hurt in one accident
2. For all people collectively hurt in one accident
3. For damage to other people's property in one accident

The liability portion of your policy usually also provides you with a lawyer to defend you if you get sued because of an auto accident. The following chart summarizes the typical liability coverage options offered by insurance companies. Insurance laws vary from state to state, so the exact amounts required are dependent upon where you live. If you can afford it, we suggest that you don't just get the entry level but go for the "good" or "even better" coverage so you have enough coverage to provide true peace of mind.

Typical Levels of Liability Coverage

What's Covered? (per accident)	Entry Level	Good	Even Better
Bodily injury, maximum covered per person	$50,000	$100,000	$250,000
Bodily injury, maximum covered for all people	$100,000	$300,000	$500,000
Property damage limit, maximum covered	$25,000	$50,000	$100,000

These three types of coverage are typically referred to using shorthand notations such as 50/100/25, 100/300/50, or 250/500/100. Be sure to confirm with your insurance company that these liability coverage figures also apply if you are in an accident caused by someone who is either uninsured or underinsured. This will ensure you have enough protection for yourself and passengers if you're in an accident with someone who does not have insurance or doesn't have enough insurance.

Auto Insurance Part 2: Physical Damage Coverage

The second part of your auto insurance is called "physical damage." As its name suggests, this part of your auto insurance protects you against physical damage that is done to your car. It has two subparts.

- *Collision* coverage pays to repair (or provide cash value for) your car if you cause an accident.
- *Comprehensive* coverage pays to repair (or provide cash value for) your car if the damage is due to other events such as fire, wind, hail, vandalism, theft, or even hitting a deer.

The price of this coverage is based on the value of your car and the amount you select for your deductible. Recall that a deductible is the amount you have to pay out of your own pocket before your insurance kicks in. The higher the deductible you select and the less expensive your car, the lower the cost of your insurance premium. We recommend you take the highest deductible you can afford to keep your premiums low. Just be sure that you can pay your deductible in the event of an accident.

HOMEOWNER'S INSURANCE

If you have a mortgage on your home, you will be required by your mortgage lender to have homeowner's insurance. Even if you own your home outright or rent, we still strongly recommend getting homeowner's (or renter's) insurance. This insurance provides property protection so that you will be reimbursed for any damage to your home and/or its contents in the event of fire, theft, or a variety of other unforeseen events. If such an event arises, you receive the value of the property less your deductible.

This insurance will also provide liability protection. Suppose a person slips on a wet floor at your house, is injured, and sues you for medical costs, lost wages, and pain and suffering. In this instance, your homeowner's or renter's policy would help protect you. Without this liability protection, you could find your future wages garnished (taken away) if your fault was deemed to have caused this harm to others.

Other Important Types of Insurance

After health, auto, and homeowner's insurance, there are three other types of insurance that you really ought to know about.

LIFE INSURANCE

The purpose of life insurance is to protect anyone you are financially responsible for in the event of your death. If you have a spouse or domestic partner who does not work, if you have dependent children, or if you are the sole provider of support for your parents or other loved ones, you should seriously consider life insurance. If you need straightforward life insurance, the only type you should buy is called term life insurance. Term life pays your stated beneficiaries a lump sum in the event of your death. Should anyone try to sell you another type of life insurance, just say no.

▷ A rough rule of thumb is to buy term life insurance in an amount equal to somewhere between five and ten times your annual income. Remember, if you don't have dependents, you don't need life insurance.

Of course, after that money is exhausted, your dependents would have to have some other source of income. Thus, for instance, if your kids are really young and your spouse is unable or unwilling to work, you might choose to buy a term life insurance policy that covers as much as fifteen times your annual income. The tradeoff, however, is the greater the payout from the policy, the higher your premium. Note that with term life insurance, the younger you are when you purchase your insurance, the less the policy will cost you per year.

DISABILITY INSURANCE

Becoming disabled is something the average healthy person gives little or no thought to. As a result, people frequently don't buy disability insurance. Yet think about it—what would happen if you were to become chronically ill and could no longer work? How would you pay your bills? Disability insurance pays some portion of your salary (typically 60 to 70 percent) if you become unable to perform your regular work duties due to a horrible accident or severe illness. Many employers offer disability insurance.

If yours does, we'd encourage you to sign up, as that's usually a very cost-effective way to get this coverage. If your employer doesn't offer this type of insurance and you have no one else on whom you could rely in an extended period of need, you should investigate this type of insurance.

> Disability policies can be costly—with annual premiums running as much as 1 to 3 percent of your salary. One way you can lower the cost is to extend the period before the policy kicks in. For instance, you might agree to a full six months of disability before your insurance kicks in, with the thought being that your emergency fund could help cover your costs until then.

UMBRELLA LIABILITY INSURANCE

An umbrella policy is a catchall, in case you are sued for a lot of money. Umbrella liability policies tend not to cost a lot. You can typically get a $1 million umbrella liability policy for under $300 per year. The reason the rates on these policies are so reasonable is that they don't kick in until after you've exceeded your regular homeowner's or auto policy coverage limits. They sit "on top," thus the name "umbrella." If you happen to have a substantial amount of savings and assets to protect, you should seriously consider this policy.

If you'd like to learn more about any particular type of insurance, go to an informational website such as *www.iii.org.* Additionally, the websites of the name-brand insurers mentioned in the next section also have a fair amount of background information.

Just Say No

Here are the kinds of insurance policies you simply *do not need*:

- **Whole, universal, or variable life insurance:** Remember, "term" is the only kind of life insurance you need—the other kinds are too expensive relative to the benefits they provide.
- **Long-term care insurance if you are under age 50:** This is something to consider in your fifties. Until then, we think you are better off using the money you would have spent on these premiums to build up your savings instead.
- **Annuities if you are under the age of 50:** In some specific situations, an annuity can make sense later in life, but you do *not* need one before age 50.
- **Specific case policies:** You do not need policies for specific kinds of coverage, such as credit card insurance, travel insurance, or disease-specific insurance (e.g., cancer insurance).

Suggestions for Purchasing Insurance

Unfortunately, buying insurance can be a real pain in the neck. The reason is that the best place to purchase one kind of insurance may not be the best place for another kind. However, a financially savvy woman needs good insurance, so let's talk about how to buy it.

Outside of your employer or college/university insurance offerings, to buy insurance, you can either go through an agent or buy directly from an insurance company. If you prefer to have someone with whom to discuss the tradeoffs inherent in an insurance policy and who can "hold your hand" come claim time, you'll be better off going with an agent. However, if you are comfortable deciding what coverage you need on your own, the flip side is that sometimes you can get a better rate going directly to the insurance company.

Where to Buy Insurance

Following are several large, reputable, brand-name insurance companies that sell the types of insurance we've discussed in this chapter. You can get contact information for any of these firms by typing the company's name into a search engine like Google or Yahoo.

- For health insurance: Aetna, Amerigroup, Blue Cross/Blue Shield, Centene, Cigna, Coventry Health Care, Health Net, Humana, Molina Healthcare, UnitedHealthcare Group, WellCare Health Plans, WellPoint
- For disability and term life insurance: Aflac, AIG, Hartford, ING, John Hancock-Manulife, Lincoln Financial, MassMutual, MetLife, Northwestern Mutual, New York Life, Prudential, TIAA-CREF, Transamerica-Aegon
- For auto, homeowner's and renter's, and umbrella insurance: Allstate, Chubb, Farmers, Geico, Hartford, Liberty Mutual, MetLife, Nationwide, Progressive, Safeco, State Farm, Travelers, USAA

Various associations and professional organizations also help members purchase insurance at more favorable group rates. These include AAA, TIAA-CREF, and USAA.

PURCHASING TIPS

When purchasing your insurance, keep in mind the following:

- **Cheaper is not always better.** You want your insurance company to be around come claim time. Our bias is toward large, reputable, brand-name firms. If in doubt, check with organizations that rate insurance companies, such as *www.ambest.com.*

- **When shopping for your initial policies, shop around.** It's best to get at least three quotes before buying. Insurance prices can vary significantly. When you compare prices, be sure to get the specific details of each policy with regard to what is and what is not covered.
- **Look for multipolicy discounts.** Once you find an insurance company that you like, consider getting your auto, homeowner's, and umbrella policies from the same firm. It's easier to keep track of your policies, and you can often get multipolicy discounts.
- **Use the Internet for some preliminary insurance comparison shopping.** There are a number of websites that specialize in helping consumers compare policies offered by different insurance companies. A few are highlighted in **APPENDIX A**.

Don't file for tiny claims. Whenever you file a claim, insurance companies consider whether they want to raise your rates. Suppose your car gets a dent and it will cost $600 to fix. We'd recommend covering that cost yourself because if you file a claim, your insurance premiums could rise by more than the cost of that small claim. Also, don't forget to consider what your deductible is. For instance, if your repairs cost $600 but your deductible is $500, you're paying for almost the entire claim out of your own pocket anyway. The purpose of insurance is to provide a safety net for big things like a fire or major accident.

Be sure that you have appropriate insurance coverage. We know that shopping for insurance is about as much fun as breaking an ankle. However, when bad times hit, having adequate insurance will add a spring to your step like you wouldn't believe. ∎

Guard Against the Unforeseen with Insurance

Evaluate your insurance needs.

Be sure you have health, auto, and homeowner's insurance. If you have dependent children, term life insurance is also a must.

It's worth going with a brand-name provider, even if it costs a little more.

You want to make sure your insurance company will still be in business if you ever need it. This is one area of your finances where cheaper is not always better.

When it comes to insurance, think Goldilocks—not too hot, not too cold.

In other words, you don't want too much insurance (that's a waste of money) or too little insurance (that will cost you money). Your goal is to get just the right amount for your personal circumstances.

CHAPTER 5

Embrace Budgeting Basics

We started off Part A by telling you to save 15 percent of your gross income for your emergency fund, big-ticket items, and retirement (recall that "gross" simply means *before* your taxes are taken out). We then reviewed three tools to help you achieve this goal: using your credit cards wisely, striving to achieve a good credit score, and protecting your financial future with key types of insurance. We have one last tool to discuss—budgeting. If you are not saving 15 percent of your gross income for your future, budgeting is an essential tool to help you figure out how to get there.

For many people, the mere sound of the "B word" conjures up thoughts of deprivation. We won't sugarcoat it: If you let them, budgets can indeed feel constraining. However, when you boil it all down, budgeting is simply a means of tracking the flow of money into and out of your life. The flow of money out of your life (that is, your *spending*) is a very important number to understand if you are having trouble saving because . . .

▷ It's your spending (as opposed to your income) over which you have the most influence on a day-to-day basis.

Having a solid understanding of the flow of money into and out of your life helps you make better choices about the inevitable tradeoffs between experiencing pleasure today and building security for tomorrow. This is powerful knowledge, and a forward-thinking woman wants to have it.

Let's Talk about Your Inflow

In order to have money to spend, you need to have income. This makes sense, right? So let's talk about that income. For most people, income consists of one or both of the following:

- Salary or wages
- Other sources of income such as dividends, interest, cash gifts, and so on

Add these together to arrive at your total gross income. For some people, this number will be constant from month to month. For others, however, this number will have a fair amount of variability. If your income is variable, an average of your monthly income over the past six months is a reasonable estimate to use.

Now Let's Talk about Your Outflow

Once you have a solid understanding of your monthly inflow, the next step is to get a complete picture of your monthly outflow. Start with your gross income and subtract your income taxes. If you're like most people, your taxes will average around 25 percent of your total income. That leaves 75 percent for three categories that we call your "Power Trio of Budgeting":

1. **Foundation expenses** are items of basic need such as groceries, shelter, and transportation. While you don't have a choice about needing these items, you *do* have some flexibility about how much to spend on them. The lower your foundation expenses, the more money you can spend on fun.
2. **Fun expenses** are the items that you *want* (as opposed to need) and that frequently bring you great joy.
3. **Future expenses,** as you might guess from the name, refer to the money you set aside for spending in the future. As we discussed in **CHAPTER 1**, this includes the savings you'll do for your emergency fund, big-ticket items, and retirement.

Your Gross Income

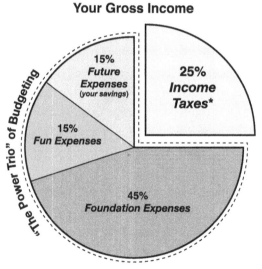

* Note, your taxes may be even higher than 25% of your gross income if you have an "above-average" income or live in an area of the country with "above-average" state/local taxes such as parts of the East and West Coasts. Since you'll still want to target 15% of your gross income for savings for Future Expenses, if your taxes are more than 25% of your gross income, your combined Fun and Foundation expenses will have to be less than 60% of your gross income.

As you can see from this pie chart, if you want to save 15 percent for the spending that you will do in the future, you will need to keep your foundation and fun expenses to 60 percent or less of your gross income. (Here's a very important note: The 25 percent tax rate we reference is for the average person, given federal tax rates at the time of this writing. If your personal taxes are higher, you'll need to spend less on foundation and fun expenses. See **CHAPTER 14** for more on taxes.)

▷ The exact mix between foundation and fun is up to you. The real key to financial security is to make sure you are saving 15 percent of your gross income for your future.

For your reference, in **APPENDIX A** we list the corresponding "Power Trio of Budgeting" targets in actual dollars for various gross income levels. This will enable you to easily see approximately how much you should be spending in each of these key areas.

Are you currently able to save 15 percent of your gross income for the future? Do you know how much of your gross income you are spending on foundation and fun expenses? If you answered "no" to either of these questions, you're not alone, and the next section will help you.

Do a Two-Month Reality Check on Your Spending

Carmen did the two-month reality check and found it incredibly eye-opening.

A Day in the Life of Carmen

Carmen is a 24-year-old administrative assistant at a nonprofit organization. She lives in Boston and makes $30,000 a year. While only three years out of college, she's already racked up hefty credit card debt on top of her student loans. Upon learning this, her older sister encouraged her to read *On My Own Two Feet*. Carmen's eyes popped wide open when she read the first chapter. She had absolutely no savings—and had no idea how to change that. Enter the reality check.

If you are not saving 15 percent of your gross income for the future, over the next two months, we'd like you to track your spending. If you've ever kept a diet diary, you'll find this is a very similar sort of thing. After two months of tracking the outflow of your cash, you'll have a pretty good sense of how much you are spending per month and where that money is going. This will enable you to see if you are blowing your budget and if so, how to identify the culprits. Here's how to track your spending:

1. Put a small notebook and a pen in your purse so that they are easily accessible.
2. As you go through the day, any time you spend money, keep track of how much you spent and on what. So, yes, when you are at the supermarket and you pay for your groceries, whip out your notebook and write down "groceries $24" or use a notepad feature on your smartphone.
3. Then, at the end of the month, go through your list and add up any expenses that would be considered part of the foundation category. Next, go back through the remaining items and total up anything else that would be considered fun.

The following chart provides a bit more color on what kinds of expenses fall into each of these categories.

Foundation Expenses	Fun Expenses
Housing: Your monthly rent or mortgage payment, homeowner's insurance, and property tax as well as other routine bills such as utilities, phone, cable, Internet	**Fun food:** Takeout, restaurants, coffees and snacks, dinner and drinks with friends, etc.
Transportation: Car payment, insurance, gas, maintenance, monthly tolls, and parking if you drive and/or your monthly bus, train, or subway pass if you take public transportation	**Fun clothing:** "*Want*" clothing, accessories, and jewelry
Basic groceries/supplies: Food, toiletries, cleaning supplies	**Entertainment:** Movies, music/concerts, DVDs or online TV/movie streaming, magazine subscriptions, books, hobbies, etc.
Debt repayment: Any mandatory payments on student loans or other debt (including credit cards)	**Personal:** Gym membership, facials, manicures, makeup, etc.
Other foundation: Health insurance, nonreimbursed medical expenses, life insurance, childcare costs, charity, and *essential* clothing	**Other:** Vacations, gifts, pets

Carmen did this reality check exercise. At the end of month one, Carmen tallied up her spending.

Carmen's Spending in Month One

Foundation: $1,400 Fun: $700 Future: $0
Monthly Grand Total: $2,100

Carmen's gross income is $2,500 a month. Once her taxes are taken out, that leaves Carmen $1,875 a month to spend, yet she is spending *$2,100*.

In doing the two-month reality check, Carmen was very surprised to find out she was spending way more than she was making. Carmen was simply doing the same things she saw her friends doing. She honestly thought she wasn't spending "that much." It turns out her spending corresponded to someone making $35,000 a year, about 16 percent more than her actual salary. Carmen was spending 56 percent of her gross income ($1,400 ÷ $2,500) on foundation expenses and another 28 percent of her gross income ($700 ÷ $2,500) on fun expenses. With 84 percent of her gross income being spent in these two areas, no wonder she was racking up hefty credit card debt and didn't have anything left over to save for her future.

It took her a while, but with this knowledge, Carmen thought long and hard about what really drove her happiness. As a result, while she decided she simply couldn't live without her snazzy gym membership or periodic gourmet javas, she chose to move into a less expensive apartment, eat out less, do her own nails, and cut back on retail therapy. She still has plenty of fun, but now she also saves some for her future.

▷ If you, like Carmen, find out that your foundation expenses or your fun expenses are too high, the next step is to take a closer look at your monthly spending records and see if there are any costs you can cut back on.

Deciding where you want to cut back will, of course, be a highly personal decision. For instance, buying the latest salon-sold hair products may make the world of difference to the happiness of one person, while it may not matter to another. That said, here are the types of general questions to ponder if you find, with our Power Trio of Budgeting guidance, that your spending is out of line.

Sample Questions to Ask Yourself When Trying to Cut Back On . . .

Foundation Expenses	Fun Expenses
Can you look for an apartment with lower rent?	Can you invite people over for a potluck dinner at your place rather than meeting at a restaurant?
If your car-related costs are high, should you trade down to a less costly model? Or rent on demand?	Can you bring your lunch to work?
Can you shop for a more competitively priced cell phone or Internet plan?	Do you read all the magazines you subscribe to?
Can you shop at a more reasonably priced grocery store?	How many new shoes, skirts, purses, earrings, etc., do you really need?

Clearly, this list is not exhaustive, but it will give you an idea of the kinds of questions to ask yourself. There are no right or wrong answers. The key is to make sure your spending reflects what really matters to *you*.

We also realize that there are many people who are truly struggling to get by—women who not only have nothing left to devote to the future but who have very little left over for fun. If you fall into this camp, we know it's extra challenging to try to figure out how to maximize your current circumstances. We realize it's not easy, and we hope this book can provide some inspiration and guidance as you work to improve your situation.

Bringing It All Together—From Budgeting to Financial Security

The financial information you gather during your reality check can also help you increase your financial security today. The reason is that you will know exactly how much you should have (or should strive to build up) in that all-important emergency fund. Recall from **CHAPTER 1** that we suggested you work to build an emergency fund that is big enough to cover at least three to six months of essential expenses (the more volatile your income or career path, the bigger the nest egg you'll want). For instance, during the reality check exercise you might discover your monthly foundation expenses are $1,500. You would then know that your ideal is to have $4,500 to $9,000 in savings to cover these essential expenses. If you don't have an emergency fund, this exercise will help highlight how much money you should strive to save.

If you find you like the feeling of empowerment that comes from understanding the flow of money into and out of your life, you may want to try a more detailed approach to budgeting. People who employ this more detailed approach often find it a useful tool to make sure their money is going toward the areas of life that bring them the most happiness. If you are interested in doing this, please see **APPENDIX A**.

As you set out on your path to saving, we strongly encourage you to set aside money to save for the future *before* you start spending for the month. This really is the single best way to make sure you don't neglect this key element of financial success. Use direct deposit or online banking features to automate the process.

The whole point of monitoring your spending is to use this information to ensure you are living within your means and saving for your future. As you learned in **CHAPTER 1**, saving for expenses you will incur in the future is absolutely essential to achieve lifelong financial success. In addition, the process of budgeting can help ensure your hard-earned dollars are going toward the areas of life that bring you the greatest joy. If, for instance, you are a person who derives most of her happiness from going to movies, concerts, and exercising in the park, it may make sense for you to spend less on an apartment or home so that you have more money to spend on activities that bring you joy outside the home. Alternatively, if you really want to buy a home, it may make sense for you to spend less money on dinners out with friends and haircuts at fancy salons so that you can set aside more money for a down payment on a house. The choice is yours.

Congratulations!

Having completed Part A, you now know the five basic tools for achieving financial success. In Part B, we'll explain how to put your savings to work by investing wisely. ■

Simple Steps for Budgeting Success

Be aware.

Know your monthly income.

Keep your target spending plan in mind.

After 25 percent is taken out of your gross income for taxes, you are aiming to allocate 60 percent to combined foundation/fun expenses and 15 percent to future expenses.

Evaluate your cash flow.

If you aren't saving 15 percent of your gross income for your future, do a two-month financial reality check to see where you are currently allocating your hard-earned dollars. Not only will this exercise help you see what changes you can make to increase your savings rate, it will also enable you to learn how much you should strive to save in your emergency fund.

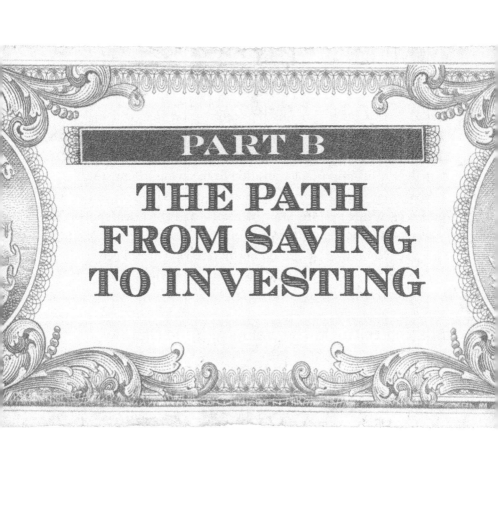

PART B

THE PATH FROM SAVING TO INVESTING

CHAPTER 6

Why Invest?

Part B of this book contains the information that will make the difference between finding yourself in a tolerable versus a great financial situation. In this section of the book, you will learn how to make the all-important transition from saving to investing.

You invest to make sure your money works as hard for you as you did for it. While keeping your money in cold hard cash may seem prudent, this chapter will explain the two reasons why this is not the case. (Note: Even if you do not have savings yet, keep reading. You'll need this knowledge once you do have savings!)

Inflation Eats Up the Value of Your Money

Wendy worked very hard to set aside some money for her future, but she thinks investments are too risky—so she's stuffing her money under her mattress. Fast-forward thirty years: Wendy is now 65 and has decided to retire. Unfortunately, the $1,000 in cash that she stuffed under her mattress will likely buy only about $400 worth of stuff in thirty years. That's less than half of what it can buy today.

Why will $1,000 in cash buy so much less thirty years from now than it will today? The culprit is inflation.

Inflation is the process by which prices go up over time. Historically, inflation has run at about 3 percent per year. This means that the average price of things has gone up about 3 percent per year. Looking forward, inflation could stay at its historical 3 percent per year average, or it could be somewhat lower or higher. The chart below shows how much $1,000 in cash today would buy thirty years from now at different rates of inflation.

What $1,000 Will Be Worth in 30 Years if Inflation Is . . .

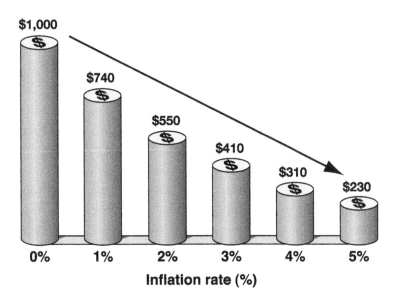

Note: Figures rounded to nearest $10.

▷ The first reason you invest is to combat the corrosive effects of inflation. Inflation is corrosive because it eats up the value of your money.

Investing, by contrast, enables you to preserve the value or the purchasing power of your money.

Investing Makes Your Money Work Harder for You

▷ The second reason to invest is that if you do it right, you'll have the opportunity to actually grow your money faster than the rate of inflation.

In plain English, this means that you will be able to make that $1,000 in savings increase fast enough that you will be able to buy even more than $1,000 worth of stuff in the future.

There are two key ways that you can make money, and everyone has access to both. The first way is the one with which most of us are all too familiar: going to work, clocking those hours, and collecting a paycheck. This is a necessary and perfectly good way to make money. However, the amount you can earn will be limited by the kind of job you have and the number of hours in a day.

The second way you can make money is to *invest* your savings. This is when you take the dollars you've saved and put that money to work for you by purchasing investments such as stocks, bonds, or real estate. If you think of yourself as the queen bee, all those dollar bills you have saved—and can invest—are your worker bees.

The reason investing can be so magical is due to a process known as compounding. Compounding means that not only does your original investment grow, but any gains from your investments also continue to grow over time. Compounding is such a powerful concept that Albert Einstein called it the "eighth wonder of the world." It works like this.

Say you have $1,000 invested in stocks, and the prices of those stocks are rising at a rate of 10 percent per year:

- At the end of the first year, you'll have $1,100. Your investment gains are $100 ($1,000 × 10%). When you add your $100 in gains to your original investment of $1,000, you get $1,100.
- At the end of the second year, you might think you'll earn another $100, thus ending up with $1,200. However, what you'll actually have is $1,210.
- Where did that extra $10 come from? Multiply the $1,100 you had at the end of the first year by 10 percent, and you get $110 in investment gains—or $10 more in investment gains compared to the end of the first year. If you add $110 in gains to your $1,100 at the end of the first year, you get $1,210.

▷ That extra $10 is the power of compounding. Compounding allows you to grow not just the money from your original investment, but also any money you've earned since that time. Think of it as profiting on your profits.

In our example, that extra $10 you got in year two thanks to compounding may not sound like a big deal. However, over time, as the process of compounding continues, those dollars add up to a lot.

In the following chart you can see what $1,000 growing at 10 percent per year would be worth over different time periods.

Growth of $1,000 at 10% per Year
for Various Time Periods

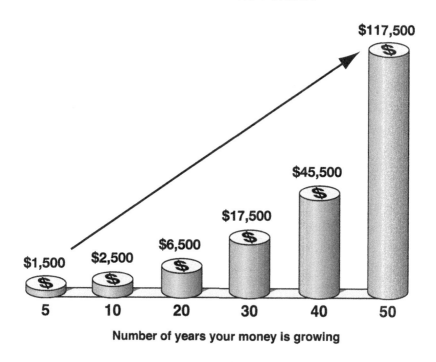

Number of years your money is growing

Note: Figures rounded to nearest $500.

This chart shows the importance of starting to save and invest as early as you can. Time is the secret to unlocking the power of compounding. Through the process of compounding you can make your money grow even faster than inflation.

Remember: Saving Is Step One and In Step Two

The difference between saving and investing is subtle but critical. Saving is the process of setting aside money to be spent in the future. Accomplishing that is no small feat. Investing is the process you can use to counteract the corrosive power of inflation and actually grow your hard-earned and hard-saved money faster than inflation. That's why Part B provides you with a roadmap to investment success. ■

You Invest Because . . .

Reason One

It may seem safe to keep your money in cash, but thanks to inflation, that's only true for the very short run.

Reason Two

Investing enables you to combat the corrosive power of inflation so your money doesn't lose its value over the long run.

Reason Three

If you invest successfully, you can actually make your money grow even faster than inflation—so you can *increase* your purchasing power in the future.

CHAPTER 7

How to Invest Your Savings

Now that we've talked about *why* you should invest, let's talk about *how* to invest your savings. Think of it as going to the gym. To get an effective workout, you must pick the right exercise equipment to achieve your fitness goals. To make sure your money gets an effective workout, you must pick the appropriate investment options for your particular situation.

How to invest your savings may seem like a very complex topic on the surface. Turn on the TV or pick up a newspaper and you'll see countless ads for all kinds of financial products. The good news, however, is that we have a "keep-it-simple-but-powerful" investment plan for you.

What you should do with your savings is driven primarily by your answer to the following question:

▷ When will you need to spend this money?

In this chapter we're going to discuss the following important topics:

- Where to park the money you'll need to spend over the next five years
- Why stocks are where the action is for money you won't need to spend for five or more years
- The simplest and most effective way to invest in stocks

Parking Money for the Next Five Years

Your main goal for money that you need to spend over the next five years is to protect it from the effects of inflation—as opposed to trying to grow it faster than inflation. Why are you only trying to match inflation and not beat it? For money you need to spend over the next five years, your main goal is to preserve its spending power. You want it to beat inflation, but at the same time you don't want to risk losing that money since you know you have to spend it. The ways in which you try to grow your money faster than inflation all involve the risk of losing money over the short term. Therefore, your goal for money you need to spend over the next five years is to shelter it from the corrosive impact of inflation. You'll do this by parking it in investment products that act like cash but provide interest rates that are just enough to offset inflation.

Specifically, we're going to touch on three options: a savings account, a money market fund/account, and a certificate of deposit (CD). Each of these options provides you with relatively easy access to your money and has a low level of risk of loss. They are all good places to put your emergency fund and any savings targeted for specific big-ticket items such as a car or home.

YOUR MONEY-PARKING OPTIONS

Here are the factors that distinguish a savings account from a money market account/fund from a CD.

- **Savings account:** A savings account is a great place to store your money when you are just getting started on your savings program. It is also where you will typically receive the lowest interest rate. (That's at a traditional bank. Internet banks sometimes offer rates on savings accounts that can be competitive with your next two options.)

- **Money market account/fund:** A money market account typically provides a higher interest rate than with your savings account, but there is often a higher minimum account size and a maximum number of monthly withdrawals. You can open a money market account at your bank. A money market fund is essentially the same thing as a money market account except that it is opened at your discount brokerage firm and typically allows more frequent withdrawals.

- **Certificate of deposit (CD):** A CD typically offers the highest interest rate among your options but at the cost of flexibility. The way a CD works is that you agree to loan out your money to the bank for a specified time period (for example, three months or three years). If you want to take your money out before the CD's agreed-upon loan period is up, you will typically forgo some interest and possibly also pay a penalty.

▷ Remember, your goal is to get the highest interest rate on your cash while also maintaining the level of flexibility you need.

Collette had been keeping her emergency fund money in an empty coffee can in her kitchen. After reading *On My Own Two Feet*, she decided to go to her local bank so she could earn some interest. She didn't have enough money to meet this bank's $1,000 minimum to participate in a money market account (which was paying 3 percent interest at that time). Collette also wanted the flexibility to access her money whenever she wanted, so a five-year CD (which was paying 4 percent interest at that time) 〉〉〉 wasn't right for her either. The optimal fit for Collette turned out to be a traditional savings account. It paid 2 percent interest and helped offset inflation while giving Collette access to her money whenever she needed it. Once she gets her savings up to $1,000, Collette is going to transfer that money to the higher-interest money market account at the same bank.

Now that we've discussed what to do with the money you need to spend during the next five years, let's talk about your longer-term savings. Examples would be savings for your retirement or your children's education.

Stocks: Where the Action Is

Broadly speaking, there are three categories of investments into which you can put the money you won't need for at least the next five years when you are trying to get it to grow faster than inflation. Those categories are stocks, bonds, and real estate.

▷ Study after study shows the secret to investment success is picking the right mix among these three categories—not finding a hot deal to invest in.

When it comes to your longer-term savings, stocks are where the action is. (This is only if you are under the age of 50—we'll explain that age caveat in **CHAPTER 8**, where we also discuss bonds and real estate.) For our purposes, when we say "stock," we mean a piece of ownership in a business that is available for purchase and sale by the general public. The price of a stock goes up or down based on investors' collective expectations of how well the underlying business will perform in the future. In addition, many companies periodically pay their stockholders a portion of the profits. These cash payouts are called dividends.

While past performance is certainly no guarantee of future returns, it never hurts to take a look at history.

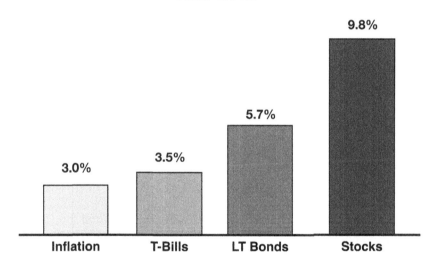

Average per Year Historical Investment Returns 1926–2012

Note: Return figures are from 1926–2012. Source data for chart includes: S&P 500 returns for stocks, U.S. Treasuries for long-term bonds and t-bills, and the consumer price index for inflation.

As you can see from this chart, over the long run, stocks have provided the highest return on investors' money.

However, when it comes to investing in stocks you'll always want to bear in mind the following: These numbers are long-run historical averages. The first thing to be aware of is that history may not repeat. The second thing to be aware of is that averages, like a good girdle, can hide a lot of jiggles. In any individual year, some of these categories fluctuated and did better or worse than the long-run average.

Sally was a very diligent saver. She wanted to buy a house, and by January 1, 2008, she had saved $40,000 for a down payment. She put all of that down payment money into the stock market with plans to pull it out one year later to buy her house. Unfortunately, 2008 was one of those years when the stock market went down, not up. That year the market declined 37 percent. Thus, at the end of the year, Sally only had $25,200 for her down payment and was unable to buy her house.

While stocks have done the best over time, they've also been the most volatile category. This means that in any individual year, stocks have tended to give investors returns that were either *much* more or *much* less than the long-run average. Because of this . . .

▷ Only put money in stocks that you can afford to leave there for at least five years.

Why five years? The rationale for that time horizon is based on history. In most historical five-year periods, stocks generated average per-year investment returns that were higher than the other investment options. However, if you really want to increase your odds of generating investment returns that beat bonds and real estate, you'll want to be even more patient. How patient? Well, ten years is good, and twenty years is even better. (See **APPENDIX B** for more details.)

Simple, Effective Stock Investing

There are two ways most people invest in stocks.

> ### *Your Options for Investing in Stocks*
>
> **Buy individual stocks.** When you buy an individual stock, you are literally buying a piece of ownership in an individual company.
>
> **Buy mutual funds.** When you buy a mutual fund, you are essentially hiring someone else (a fund manager) to buy a "basket" of stocks for you. A mutual fund is a bucket of money that is used to purchase individual stocks on behalf of the people who contributed the money. The benefit of this approach is that with a relatively small amount of money, you can get pieces of ownership in many different companies. This helps lower your risk. It also involves a lot less work on your part than researching individual companies to figure out which ones to own.

Mutual funds come in two broad types. The first type is what's called an actively managed mutual fund. Here, professional fund managers use different strategies to decide what stocks to buy and what stocks to sell in their respective mutual funds each day. There are more than 7,000 different actively managed mutual funds in the United States. When you invest in actively managed mutual funds, you are essentially betting on the skill of the professional fund manager.

The second type of mutual fund is what's called a passively managed index fund. With an index fund, the basket of stocks is decided upfront. There is not a lot of daily buying and selling going on. Managers of index funds only buy or sell stocks when a major event happens, such as one company buying another or a strategic change is made to the composition of the index. When you invest in an index fund, you are essentially investing in stocks as an overall investment category without trying to bet on the skill of an individual money manager.

▷ Believe it or not, index funds have historically done better than more than 80 percent of active, professionally managed mutual funds.

That means that based on history, you have a greater than 80 percent chance of making more money with an index fund than with an actively managed mutual fund. Yes, this includes all those sexy funds that just had a blockbuster year and are being touted in the financial press. In fact, study after study shows the worst time to put money into an actively managed mutual fund is right after it has a hot streak.

▷ If you want to keep your financial life simple, we *strongly* recommend that you use index funds to invest in stocks.

Index funds have another important advantage. They cost *much* less than actively managed mutual funds. This may not seem like a big deal, but as you can see from Hanna's experience, cost is a very, very big deal.

Hanna has never been a big fan of looking at the prices of things, particularly when it comes to financial products. She has her hard-earned $10,000 in savings invested in an actively managed mutual fund that she heard about from a friend. It charges a yearly fee (called an "expense ratio") of 2.5 percent. That fee sounded perfectly reasonable to Hanna, so ⟩⟩⟩

she never gave it a second thought. What Hanna didn't realize is the true financial impact that fee had on her investment over time:

Hanna's pricey actively managed mutual fund: $10,000 increasing at 10 percent a year for thirty years, with an annual fee of 2.5 percent, grows to $87,500.

If Hanna had gone instead with an index fund: $10,000 increasing at 10 percent a year for thirty years with an annual fee of 0.5 percent grows to *$152,000.*

When you invest in mutual funds, what you ultimately get to take home is the money that's left over after fees are paid. The lower the fee, the more of your money you get to keep.

So, an index fund typically has better performance and costs less than an actively managed mutual fund—what a deal! Which index fund is right for you? Here is our keep-it-simple-but-powerful action plan:

▷ For money you don't need to spend for at least five years: Put it in an S&P 500 index fund.

As you venture out in pursuit of investment success, remember this: If history is any guide, our recommended investment plan will put you ahead of the vast majority of investors. This includes all of the so-called sophisticated and super-complex approaches to investing. When it comes to investing, simple can be extremely powerful. That said, we know you may have more questions about this process. Thus, we've dedicated **CHAPTER 8** to answering frequently asked questions about investing in stocks, bonds, and real estate. ∎

What Exactly Is an S&P 500 Index Fund?

An S&P 500 index fund is an easy and highly effective way to invest money in stocks. "S&P" stands for "Standard & Poor's," the company that decides which stocks go in this particular basket. When you invest in an S&P 500 index fund, you are basically buying a small amount of ownership in 500 of the largest publicly traded U.S. companies (think Apple, ExxonMobil, and General Electric). If you invest your money in an S&P 500 index fund, you get to own a small piece of 500 different companies that operate in a variety of industries. Many of these companies sell their products and services not just in the United States but all around the globe—so you are also getting some geographic diversification. (If you want to get a little more advanced and add in smaller companies and international exposure, see suggestions in **CHAPTER 8**.)

How to Invest Your Money

Option One

For money that you must spend in the next five years, your goal is to protect it from inflation by keeping it in a savings account, a money market account/fund, or a certificate of deposit (CD).

Option Two

For money that you will be spending more than five years from now, your goal is to try to grow it even faster than inflation. You have three basic types of investments with which to do this: stocks, bonds, and real estate.

Option Three

If you have at least five years *and* you are under the age of 50, our recommendation is to invest in stocks via an S&P 500 index fund. We think this is a highly effective keep-it-simple choice.

CHAPTER 8

Frequently Asked Investing Questions

Investing is a topic that raises all sorts of questions. This chapter provides straightforward answers to some of the most common questions that arise when it comes to:

- Investing in stocks
- Investing in bonds
- Investing in real estate

Investing in Stocks

Q Susan, age 35, asks: "I think the future is all about small and medium-sized U.S.-based companies as well as large international companies. Can't I get an index fund that will focus on these types of companies in addition to large U.S.-based companies?"

A Yes, if you are willing to put in a bit more effort, you can create a mix of index funds that will enable you to capitalize on virtually any investment theme you want. If you want to focus on the trends Susan mentioned, we'd recommend the following plan.

> ### Some Like It Small, Medium, and Large (Here and Abroad)
>
> - Put one-third of your money in an extended market index fund. This will give you exposure to small and medium-sized U.S.-based companies.
> - Put one-third of your money in an S&P 500 index fund. This will give you exposure to large U.S.-based companies.
> - Put one-third of your money in an international index fund. This will give you exposure to large, established companies headquartered in developed markets outside of the United States.
>
> If you are interested in implementing this strategy, see **APPENDIX B** for more details.

That said, we would be remiss if we didn't point out the following information. While historically small and medium-sized U.S.-based companies have done even better than large U.S.-based companies (and, more recently, international companies have also done quite well), both categories have also been much more volatile than large U.S.-based companies. Do not attempt this approach unless you are willing to ride that roller coaster.

Q Wendy, age 31, asks: "I read that ETFs are a great way to invest because of their low cost. What's the difference between an ETF and an index fund?"

A "ETF" stands for "exchange-traded fund." As with an index fund, an ETF is essentially a static basket of stocks. However, the main difference is that ETFs trade all day long (just like a stock), while index funds get priced at the end of a trading day. In return for the benefit of being able to trade throughout the day, ETFs require you to pay a fee, called a commission, each time you buy or sell. These fees can get costly if you invest small sums of money at a time (for example, $100 each paycheck). Given this and the fact that we don't see why a long-term investor would need the benefit of trading intra-day, we prefer index funds. That said, there are times when an ETF can make sense if you are willing to increase your investment complexity.

Q Gretchen, age 27, asks: "My brother owned this actively managed mutual fund that went up over 40 percent last year. Why shouldn't I buy a mutual fund like that one?"

A Since you invest in stocks for the long run, it's not enough to buy last year's hot mutual fund. The issue with actively managed mutual funds is that finding a good one is like looking for a needle in a haystack. There are some truly excellent ones out there, but it requires significant effort on your part to identify them. Unless you are really into the process of learning about investing and researching active money managers, we strongly urge you to stick with index funds.

Q Jessica, age 23, asks: "What if I *really* want to buy an individual stock?"

A We're not opposed to your setting aside a *tiny* portion of your money (that means less than 5 percent) to do this, as long as you mentally think about this as gambling money. Your chosen stock(s) may go up, but they also may go way down. Unless you plan to devote yourself to becoming a stock-picking expert, we encourage you to think long and hard about this option.

The easiest way to buy individual stocks is through a discount broker. You can place an order online or over the phone, and you will be charged a commission (a fee) for this service. If you do decide to purchase individual stocks, understand that knowing what to buy is only half the game. It is just as hard, or harder, to know if and when to sell. Remember that the cards are stacked against you if you choose this route. The evidence is clear that even the vast majority of professional investors can't beat the market consistently.

▷ Buying individual stocks is *not* for the faint of heart.

If you decide to buy actively managed mutual funds or individual stocks, please be sure to see **APPENDIX B**, where we list the two classic pitfalls to avoid.

Investing in Bonds

Q Colleen, age 20, asks: "My parents own bonds. What are they?"

A A bond represents a loan to a company or a governmental entity for a specific period of time. When you own a bond, you are essentially loaning money to one of these entities. In return for doing so, you have the opportunity to make money in two ways:

1. You receive periodic interest payments. These interest payments typically are constant, or fixed. This is why people sometimes call bonds "fixed income."

2. If you hold the bond until the loan period is up, you will also receive a larger sum of money at the end of that period (technically called a "return of principal").

The return of principal is where the notion of bonds being safe investments comes from. *However,* if you sell a bond before its loan period is up, the amount of money you get back may be more or less than how much you paid for the bond, depending on where interest rates are when you sell.

Q Sarah, age 30, asks: "When should I buy bonds?"
A For someone your age, stocks are where the action is. However, you will not want this action for your whole life. Our advice is that once you hit age 50, it's time to start shifting money into bonds. Once you hit age 50, you are typically at a stage in your life and career where preserving your money for retirement starts to become more important than trying to grow it faster than inflation. Here's a rough rule of thumb for women, who have statistically longer life spans than men:

▷ Starting at age 50, the percentage of your portfolio to keep in stocks is no more than 110 minus your age. Bonds (or cash equivalents) are appropriate for the rest of your portfolio.

That means at age 50, you'll want no more than 60 percent of your money in stocks:

110 − 50 [age] = 60 [percent of money in stocks]

The rest of your money should be in bonds—or in cash if you'll be spending it in the very near term. (Men have statistically shorter expected life spans. After age 50, the portion of their portfolios invested in stocks should typically not exceed 100 minus their age.)

Investing in Real Estate

Q Karen, age 34, asks: "I really like the idea of real estate because it's something I can see and touch as opposed to stocks. What do you think?"

A We frequently hear people talking about wanting to own property for rental income. It sure sounds good on the surface—buy rental property and get steady rental income back in return. However, many people neglect to take into consideration all the expenses that accompany that rental income (such as property tax, insurance, maintenance, and the cost and time of upkeep). These costs end up reducing your true investment return after expenses.

In fact, over the long run, once you factor in these associated expenses, real estate returns tend to just barely beat inflation. (Recall the chart of historical annual investment returns in **CHAPTER 7**.) Unless you want to be in the business of real estate or feel you have particular insight into a property's potential for price appreciation, we feel that ownership of your own home is more than enough exposure to real estate for the average person.

Q Lauren, age 39, asks: "I hear that 'leverage' can really help you make a killing on real estate. Is that true?"

A What Lauren is referring to is that most people have to borrow money (that is, take out a mortgage) to purchase real estate. "Leverage" simply means borrowing money. For example, if you buy a $200,000 house with 10 percent down, you're investing only $20,000 of your own cash. You borrow the remaining $180,000 from the bank. When you're ready to sell your house, if it's gone up, things look very good. For instance, suppose you sell your house for $220,000—that is, for $20,000 more than you paid for it. You would have made a stunning profit of 100 percent on the money *you* invested. That's the math people are referring to when they gush about the power of real estate leverage.

What many people forget, however, is that real estate prices don't always go up. What if that house sold for $180,000 instead? Then you'd have a *loss* of 100 percent of your investment. Additionally, this doesn't factor in the transaction costs associated with buying and selling your house or your interest payments—costs that can easily reach 10 percent of the price of a home and bite deep into those heady gains.

Deidre doesn't like to take a lot of risk. She always wears her seatbelt and flosses her teeth twice a day. Deidre thought it would be much safer to put her savings in a rental property than something more "exotic" like shares of stocks. She bought a fixer-upper house near a university campus with the plan of renting it out to students. She figured the steady stream of rental income would provide her with a lifelong safety net. Then she discovered the reality of being a landlady—6 A.M. calls to unclog the toilet, tenants who didn't always pay on time, and property taxes and insurance costs that sometimes went up faster than she could increase her rent. Deidre's rental property has now gone from "safe haven" to "money pit."

If you want to invest in real estate or learn more about the nuances of investing, check out **APPENDIX B**.

Congratulations, you now know *how* to invest your money. In **CHAPTER 9**, we'll discuss *where* to store the money you will save and invest for your retirement. See the end of **CHAPTER 1** if you need a refresher on where to store your savings for your emergency fund and big-ticket items. ∎

The Secret to Successful Investing Is to Keep It Simple

Secret One

If you want to keep your investment life simple (a goal we strongly support), we believe that owning an S&P 500 index fund is a highly effective way to invest in stocks.

Secret Two

If you want more investment complexity, you can purchase index funds that are focused on all kinds of market sectors and geographies.

Secret Three

We generally do not recommend that you invest in bonds until you reach age 50. Before that, with five or more years on your side, the odds are that you'll do better with stocks over the long run. As for real estate, we feel that for the vast majority of people, ownership of a home is more than enough exposure to this investment category.

CHAPTER 9

Super-Size Your Retirement Savings

In **CHAPTER 1** we said your goal is to save 15 percent of your gross income, with at least two-thirds of that (that is, 10 percent of your gross income) going toward your retirement savings. Thus, the majority of the money you'll be saving and investing will be money earmarked for your retirement.

There are two types of special retirement accounts that enable you to reap tax benefits: tax-deferred accounts and tax-exempt accounts. Tax-deferred accounts allow you to push off paying taxes until retirement. Tax-exempt accounts allow you to put in after-tax dollars today and never pay taxes again. These tax-advantaged retirement accounts are a big deal because . . .

▷ Tax-advantaged retirement accounts allow you to end up with *more* money at retirement.

You can access these types of retirement accounts in two ways:

- Through your employer-sponsored retirement savings plan
- Through an individual retirement account (IRA)

In this chapter we will discuss what a financially savvy woman needs to know about both of these options. We will also review frequently asked questions about retirement savings.

Tax-Deferred vs. Tax-Exempt Retirement Accounts

- **Tax-deferred:** In these types of accounts, contributions are generally made from your salary *before* taxes are taken out. Additionally, the investment income you earn is not taxed while in your account. This allows you to reinvest 100 percent of your investment gains. You will, however, have to pay taxes on both your before-tax contributions and on your investment gains when you withdraw that money to spend in your retirement. These types of accounts are attractive because you are able to delay having to pay income taxes for many years. As a result, you will build a much larger retirement nest egg than what you'd end up with in a taxable account.
- **Tax-exempt:** In these types of accounts, contributions are made from your salary after taxes are paid. The benefit of this type of account is that you pay no income tax when you withdraw your money in retirement. In other words, you pay no additional taxes on your contributions and no taxes on your investment gains.

Employer-Sponsored Retirement Savings Plans

If you work for a medium or large organization, there's a good chance your organization offers an employer-sponsored retirement savings plan. Most firms offer a tax-deferred employer-sponsored retirement savings plan (although a few have started to offer a tax-exempt version, called a Roth). While this type of plan can go by different names—such as 401(k) plan, 403(b) plan, 457 plan, and Thrift Savings Plan—they all work in pretty much the same manner.

If you're offered a traditional tax-deferred plan, you get to decide how much money from your before-tax salary you want to contribute to your retirement savings. You can contribute up to the maximum limit set by your employer. Your employer takes the amount of money you choose out of your paycheck and places it into your personal retirement savings account. From the set of choices offered by your employer, you then decide how you want your money invested.

In addition to being tax-advantaged, there are two more reasons why your employer-sponsored retirement savings plan is so great:

1. **Employer-sponsored plans are an easy way to save money for retirement.** Once you sign up for the plan, your money is taken out of your salary automatically, before you even receive your paycheck. Since you never really see that money, you are not tempted to spend it.
2. **You may have the opportunity to get free money from your employer.** Some companies will match a percentage of the amount that you contribute, up to a specified level—typically the first 3 to 6 percent of your salary that you contribute. For example, if you contribute $1 out of your salary, your employer might put an additional $0.50 into your retirement account (some employers may even match with a full $1). This match is a totally free gift to you. Amazing, right?

If you don't know whether your employer offers a retirement savings plan, check with your supervisor or human resources department. If you know you don't have access to this type of plan, you can skip to the next section—your IRA will be your primary retirement savings vehicle.

Maya makes $50,000 a year. She contributes 10 percent of her gross salary (or $5,000) to her employer-sponsored retirement savings plan over the course of the year. On top of this, Maya's employer matches $0.50 on the dollar on the first 6 percent of her salary that she contributes to the plan. This means that in addition to the $5,000 a year Maya contributes from her own salary, her employer contributes *another* $1,500 (6% × $50,000 × $0.50). As a result, Maya actually saves $6,500 a year, or 13 percent, of her gross salary. Put another way, she makes a 30 percent return on her savings before she even invests it!

The following graph shows what a big deal this "match" can be over the long run.

How a $0.50 Match Can Turn into $368,000: Maya's pool of savings at retirement

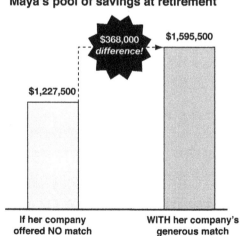

Note: Each bar assumes that beginning at age 25 Maya contributes $5,000 a year to her employer-sponsored retirement savings plan and that her investments grow at 10% per year up to age 59½.

While an extra $0.50 or $1 may not sound like a windfall, over time your employer's matching contribution can be worth *a lot* of money. If it's offered at your company, do all you can to contribute enough to receive the maximum amount of your employer's match. This truly is free money, so you don't want to pass it up.

Now, to fully benefit from your employer-sponsored retirement savings plan, you must be aware of and heed the two following critical caveats.

CAVEAT #1

YOU'VE PICKED THE RESTAURANT, NOW YOU MUST ORDER OFF THE MENU

After you have signed up to participate in your employer's plan, you must now order wisely off your plan's menu of investment options to ensure your money works as hard as possible for you. The majority of employers offer a "menu" with anywhere from five to fifteen different investment choices. A natural tendency is to just put a little bit of money in every investment option available to you. However, this is precisely what you do not want to do, for a couple of reasons.

▷ While it may seem logical, it's actually not a wise strategy to spread your money across all of the investment options offered in your employer-sponsored retirement savings plan.

The reason is twofold. First, many of the available options—ranging from money market funds to bond funds—are too conservative for retirement money that you are not planning to touch for many years. Second, many options charge unnecessarily high fees. If you are under age 50, a smart approach is to follow the investment advice from the previous two chapters and put 100 percent of your money in stocks, ideally via index funds.

> If your plan doesn't offer index funds, you'll need to choose an actively managed mutual fund that most closely resembles the index fund you prefer. See **APPENDIX B** for help in choosing the right actively managed fund.

CAVEAT #2

THINK LONG AND HARD BEFORE TAKING OUT A LOAN AGAINST YOUR ACCOUNT

While you can't take money out of your account before age 59½ without paying hefty penalties, some companies will allow you to borrow money against your balance for special circumstances, such as for a down payment on a home or to pay emergency medical bills.

▷ Only borrow from your employer-sponsored retirement savings plan if you are facing a *real* emergency.

Individual Retirement Accounts (IRAs)

An IRA is the second type of tax-advantaged retirement account that can super-size your retirement savings. You open up an IRA on your own at the financial institution of your choice, instead of through your employer (see **APPENDIX A** for a list of the three large discount firms). You must have sufficient income generated from work to contribute to an IRA. If you are a stay-at-home spouse, an IRA is still an important account for you to know about. If you and your spouse file your taxes jointly, and your working spouse earns at least the total amount you want to contribute to both of your IRAs in a given year, each of you can fund your IRA.

▷ IRAs come in three basic types: Roth, traditional, and rollover.

THE ROTH IRA

The Roth is our favorite type of IRA. This is a tax-exempt account. You put *after*-tax dollars into it, but then you will never have to pay taxes again. The Roth IRA is also very flexible, making it pretty close to the financial equivalent of the perfect pair of jeans. You can withdraw the money you contribute to this account at any time, without paying taxes or penalties. However, taxes and penalties do apply if you withdraw investment gains before you are 59½ years old. This means your Roth IRA can serve as a backup emergency fund of last resort. While this is good to know, only consider this option if you are facing an emergency situation.

▷ If you qualify, the Roth IRA is the best kind to have. As of 2013, if you are single and make $112,000 or less a year (or if you are married, filing jointly, making $178,000 or less) you can contribute to a Roth IRA and experience its full benefits.

In 2013, you are allowed to put up to $5,500 a year into a Roth IRA. Both the income level to qualify for a Roth IRA as well as contribution limits may increase in the future. (For current limits, search the Internet for "20XX Roth IRA income limit" (XX stands for the current year) or "20XX Roth IRA contribution limit.")

THE TRADITIONAL IRA

This is a tax-deferred account. Your contribution, however, may be before- or after-tax depending on two factors: (1) Your total income after certain adjustments, and (2) Whether you (or your spouse) are covered by an employer's pension plan.

A traditional IRA is less attractive than a Roth IRA in that you have to pay taxes on all the money you withdraw from it after retirement—any before-tax contributions as well as all investment gains. Furthermore, a traditional IRA does not allow the same flexibility as a Roth IRA in terms of serving as an emergency fund of last resort. This is because you cannot take out the money you originally contributed on a penalty-free basis the way you can with a Roth IRA. Consequently, we favor the Roth IRA. However, if you have the pleasant problem of making too much money to qualify for a Roth IRA, the traditional IRA is still an excellent way to take advantage of tax-deferred retirement savings.

> While not as powerful as the Roth IRA, a traditional IRA is still an excellent way to save for retirement.

For 2013, the traditional IRA has the same $5,500 contribution limit as the Roth IRA. This amount is also expected to increase in the future. (Type "20XX Traditional IRA contribution limits" into a search engine to find current limits.)

If you are self-employed, you can open a version of the traditional IRA called a SEP (for "simplified employee pension") IRA account. A SEP works like a traditional IRA but has higher contribution limits since it will be your primary retirement savings vehicle.

THE ROLLOVER IRA

If you leave a job where you participated in an employer-sponsored retirement savings plan, you'll have to decide what to do with your money. You have four choices:

1. Cash out your IRA and pay stiff penalties.

2. Leave the 401(k) with your former employer.

3. "Roll over" your 401(k) to your new employer's plan.

4. Roll your 401(k) over into a (traditional tax-deferred) rollover IRA.

▷ We strongly recommend that you open up a rollover IRA and have your money transferred directly from your previous employer to this new account. Doing this is a smart financial move that will give you *much* more control over your money.

If you move your money into a rollover IRA, you will be able to make sure it goes into the index fund you prefer, as opposed to being limited by the investment options offered by your old or new employer. If you are thinking of changing jobs, check out **APPENDIX B** to learn how to move your money into a rollover IRA.

Frequently Asked Questions about Retirement Savings

Q Ria, age 24, asks: "I contribute to my employer-sponsored retirement savings plan up to the point of the maximum match; however, I want to save more. Should I increase the percentage of my salary that I contribute to my employer-sponsored retirement savings plan, or start funding an IRA?"

A Increasing the percentage of your salary that you contribute to your employer's plan is the simplest, most straightforward approach for additional retirement savings. That said, if you qualify for a Roth IRA, we recommend a slightly different strategy. We suggest that you next fully fund your Roth IRA account up to the maximum allowed. Your Roth IRA is a more attractive option due to its ability to serve as an emergency fund of last resort, the added boost of tax-free withdrawals in retirement, and the fact that you have more investment options so you can find those index funds. If, however, you don't qualify for a Roth, then tell your employer to increase the percentage saved from your paycheck.

If you still have money to save after you have fully funded your Roth IRA, increase the percentage saved from your paycheck.

Q Penelope, age 38, asks: "If I'm self-employed, how do I prioritize my retirement savings?"

A If you qualify for one, fully fund your Roth IRA first, and then contribute as much as you can to your SEP IRA. If your income is so high that you don't qualify for a Roth IRA, put the most you can into a SEP IRA.

Q Nadine, age 21, asks: "Where should I open my IRA?"

A Recall from the end of **CHAPTER 1** that we suggested opening a discount brokerage account for your emergency fund and big-ticket item savings. That same discount brokerage firm is the ideal place to open your IRA. Having just one other institution housing your money outside of your local bank simplifies your financial life.

Q Thalia, age 37, asks: "I know that pushing off taxes between now and retirement is a good thing, but can you summarize the tax status of deposits and withdrawals for each account?"

A The rules and regulations of tax-advantaged accounts can make even a certified public accountant's head spin. The following chart summarizes, as of this writing, the different types of accounts, the tax treatment of the money going into the accounts, and the tax treatment of the money coming out of the accounts when you retire. ■

	Employer-Sponsored Retirement Savings Plan	Roth IRA or Roth 401(k)	Traditional IRA	SEP IRA	Rollover IRA
Your Contributions	Before-tax	After-tax	Before-tax and/or after-tax*	Before-tax	Before-tax
Your Withdrawals	You pay regular income tax on *any* withdrawals	You pay *no* taxes on any withdrawals	You pay regular income tax on *any before-tax* contributions and on your investment gains	You pay regular income tax on *any* withdrawals	You pay regular income tax on *any* withdrawals

*You contribute on a before-tax basis if: (a) you (or your spouse) are not covered by an employer pension plan or (b) if you (or your spouse) are covered by an employer pension plan but your income is below an allowable threshold. You contribute on an after-tax basis if you (or your spouse) are covered by an employer pension plan and your income is above the allowable threshold. Note that your contributions can be partly before-tax and partly after-tax depending on your income.

Push Off Uncle Sam and Super-Size Your Retirement Savings

Your employer-sponsored retirement savings plan and IRAs super-size your retirement savings by pushing off Uncle Sam (in the form of the tax man). This means you end up with *more money* when you reach retirement.

If you are eligible to participate in an employer-sponsored retirement savings plan, do everything you can to at least contribute up to the point of your employer's maximum match.

Keep in mind your end goal of saving at least 10 percent of your gross income in your tax-advantaged retirement accounts.

CHAPTER 10

Prioritize Your Financial Plan

When it comes to personal finance, one size rarely fits all. At the same time, there are a few basic steps from which virtually everyone can benefit. So let's put together a financial plan that works for you. Do you find yourself wondering about any of these questions?

- What comes first—building my emergency fund or saving for retirement?
- How do my student loans, credit card, and other debt factor into the equation?
- When do I save for a down payment on a house?

Well, wonder no more. In this chapter we provide a straightforward roadmap for dealing with these common questions.

Prioritizing Your Financial Plan

The seven-step process we provide in this chapter will help you prioritize your financial plan and put you firmly on the road to financial success. This is the chapter that pulls together all that you've learned so far in this book. By taking these steps, you will also be taking the actions necessary to make your financial success a reality:

1. **Make the minimum required debt payments on all of your outstanding debt.** This is absolutely vital to protecting your credit score.
2. **Save $2,000 as a "starter" emergency fund.** According to a study by the Consumer Federation of America, this is the average amount of unexpected expenses in a given year.
3. **Contribute to your employer-sponsored retirement savings plan up to the maximum point of your employer's match.** This is literally free money, so do all you can to take advantage of it.
4. **Continue to build up your emergency fund to cover three to six months of your foundation expenses.** The one thing in life you can expect is the unexpected; this fund will give you the financial flexibility to roll with the punches. (If you need a refresher on foundation expenses, please refer to **CHAPTER 5**.)
5. **If you have any credit card debt, pay more than your monthly minimum payment.** Paying off credit card debt is one of the *best* investments you can make. Increasing your monthly payments according to the schedule below will dramatically reduce the time it takes to rid yourself of your debt.

Your additional credit card debt payment *every* month should be *at least* $50 to $150 above your minimum required monthly payment. If your debt is:

- **$5,000 or less:** Pay at least an extra $50 every month.
- **Between $5,000 and $10,000:** Pay at least an extra $100 every month.
- **Over $10,000:** Pay at least an extra $150 every month.

Note: Pay the extra amount on your debt with the highest interest rate first.

6. **If you are ready to buy a home, it's time to save for a down payment.** Your home down payment is one of the largest big-ticket items you'll ever make, so make it a savings priority.

7. **If you aren't ready or don't want to buy a house or have already bought one, then keep saving for your retirement.** The dollars you save early on for your retirement are the most powerful as they have the most time to grow for you. Recall from **CHAPTER 9** that there are two special types of tax-advantaged retirement accounts (employer-sponsored retirement savings plans and IRAs) to use to super-size your retirement savings.

Frequently Asked Questions

Q Vera, age 23, asks: "What about saving for other big-ticket items, such as a car?"

A If you need to buy a car because you don't have one and you *must have* a car to get to work, then consider buying the least expensive, but safe, car you can before starting the seven-step process in this chapter. If you simply *want* a car (or want a nicer car), we'd urge you to make sure you are meeting your savings goals for retirement first and then save for a down payment on your (next) car. See **CHAPTER 13** for more on buying a car.

Q Sandra, age 36, asks: "How about saving for my upcoming wedding?"

A Again, we'd advise you to meet your retirement savings goals first, and then save for a wedding. Remember that the retirement dollars you save in your early years are the most valuable because they have the most time to grow. Your wedding is a day you'll want to remember forever, but not because you blew your financial future on it.

Q Carrie, age 42, asks: "What about my children's education? How do I prioritize that?"

A If you have kids, you very well may want to help them pay for their college education. However, it's important to save for that goal *after* you have set aside money for your own retirement. It has been said that kids can get scholarships for college, but adults don't get scholarships for retirement. If you are interested in helping your children pay for their college education, check out the resources we list in **APPENDIX B**.

▷ As with all financial advice, your personal circumstances and your personal priorities will dictate the degree to which you follow this roadmap.

For instance, if the thought of your credit card debt is making you nauseated, you may choose to focus first on paying down all of your debt before saving for retirement to give you more peace of mind. Alternatively, you may decide that you really want to fully fund your Roth IRA before you start saving for a down payment on a house. The choice, as always, is yours.

By following this roadmap, you'll be on your way to financial security. The last step in your journey is to get tactical about some potentially tough real-life situations. We discuss how to do this in the next (and final) section of the book. With this last set of tools, you will have the basic building blocks to create the financial life that's right for you. As a result, you can build a life free of financial stress and focus instead on turning your dreams into reality. ∎

Grappling with the Competing Demands on Your Money

Always pay at least the minimum required on *all* of your outstanding debt/bills *and* save $2,000 as a starter emergency fund.

If you have the option, do all you can to contribute up to the maximum point of your company's employer-sponsored retirement savings plan match. This literally is free money, so you don't want to pass it up.

Never forget that paying off high-interest debt is one of the best investments you can make in your future.

PART C

THE STRATEGIES FOR REAL-LIFE SITUATIONS

CHAPTER 11

Your Student Loans

For years, higher education was considered a one-way ticket to the American Dream. The math of higher education made excellent sense. By investing in education, you would see your earnings grow and your career options blossom. As such, student loan debt has traditionally been considered "good debt." For the majority of career paths, taking on student loans generated a very positive return on that investment. This could be seen statistically, both in the significantly higher earnings for individuals with college degrees versus high school diplomas, and in the fact that up until around ten years ago, student loan debt struggles were fairly isolated.

Fast forward to today and it is a very different story. According to the Institute for College Access & Success' Project on Student Debt, two-thirds of the class of 2011 held student loans upon graduation. The average loan outstanding was an eye-popping $26,600. When you compare that to the average starting salary for the class of 2011 of $41,000, you can see this is quite a financial burden to be carrying right out of school. Today, millions of people are struggling with student loans.

That struggle is understandable. Let's say Sally is earning that average of $41,000 a year and takes home $30,750 after taxes (assuming a 25 percent effective tax rate). Sally is determined to pay off her student loans and is quite disciplined about it. She sets aside 10% of her after-tax salary to pay down her student loans. At that pace, to pay off her $26,600 in student loans, which carry a 7 percent interest rate, it will take her fourteen years to become debt free!

Most students don't think about the math of student loan payback up front and what that will mean for their standard of living given their chosen career. The goal of this chapter is to try and change that. We want you to think about your loan repayment plan as part of the total equation of applying to schools.

If you are a recent graduate reading this book, you may be nodding your head in an all-too-familiar feeling of understanding. Before we go any further, we want to say that no matter where you are now, you went to school for a good reason: You went to enrich your mind. The knowledge you have gained from school is an asset no one can take away from you. The way you choose to put it to work in the future can bring you great joy. So even though you may be struggling with student loan debt, you know that it wasn't as if you went on a spending spree at a high-end department store for frivolous items you didn't need.

That said, times have changed and we need a new way to think about when to pay and how much to pay for education. In this chapter, we help you think about how much is reasonable to borrow for education. If you already have student loans and are struggling with them, we will explain your basic options for loan relief.

Heading Off To School? Consider Our Higher Education Rule of Thumb

Student loans are serious business. Once you borrow that money, you are legally on the hook for that debt. So you want to think long and hard before agreeing to take on any student loans. A rough rule of thumb we find helpful when thinking about how much is "too much" to spend on education is this: Don't take out more loans than what you think you will make as your average yearly salary over the ten years after school.

That's a mouthful, so let's break it down. Say you want to pursue a career in marketing and you think you will earn an average of $50,000 a year for the first ten years that you work in this career. Now say you have been accepted to a really great private college where the average room, board, and tuition total $40,000 a year (adding up to $160,000 for four years). So here's the question: Would having $160,000 in loans be reasonable if you expect to earn $50,000? Unfortunately, probably not. Why?

Let's say your interest rate on your student loans is somewhere between 4 percent (the current low end for some government loans as of this writing), and 12 percent-plus (which it can be for private loans). If you set aside 10 percent of your take-home income a year—which is no small dent in your cash flow—it would take anywhere from twelve to more than twenty-five years to pay down that debt. If you apply less than 10 percent of your income to student loan payments it will take even longer to pay off that debt.

Thinking about paying back your student loans in the context of the Power Trio of Budgeting helps explain how something that seems on the surface to be so good (getting an education) can quickly turn into a financial noose by limiting the money you have to spend in other areas. The money has to come from somewhere and that 10 percent takes a big bite out of the Power Trio of Budgeting pie. If your student loan repayments are much more than 10 percent of your take-home pay, it will put undue financial stress on your shoulders. Time and again, we've seen this student loan–induced financial anxiety create dread and even regret for having taken on a mountain of student loan debt.

You may be asking why we are suggesting that you compare your debt to a ten-year average income. The reason is that some career paths have income trajectories that start out very low but can grow to large numbers. If we just compared student loans to the starting salary, we wouldn't get an accurate picture of just how powerful that education will be over the long run. For instance, a new doctor in residency may make $30,000 a year but make over $200,000-plus ten years out. That's why we suggest the ten-year average as the way to measure your income.

Importantly, this is not a hard and fast rule. You may willingly choose to spend more on your education for a specific reason. For example, you may be a gifted musician and get into a top private school for music. The loans you take out may be quite large in relationship to your future earnings. But the joy that you will receive from pursuing that career path is so great you are willing to make the tradeoff of having less to spend in either your foundation or fun categories. The key is that you are making a conscious tradeoff.

Types of Student Loans

When applying for student loans, there are two basic types that you can use: government loans and private loans (i.e., commercial loans issued by banks). To apply for a government loan, you will need to fill out the Free Application for Federal Student Aid, also known as FAFSA. You can get this application at *www.fafsa.ed.gov*. There are two basic types of federal loans: **>>>**

- **Direct loans:** the U.S. government is your lender
- **Perkins loans:** your school is your lender

Of the total in student loans outstanding, right now roughly 85 percent are government loans and 15 percent are private loans. Government loans nearly always have lower interest rates and more options around repayment than private loans. We strongly suggest you research and exhaust all government loan options before entertaining the idea of private loans.

What to Do if You're Struggling to Repay Student Loans

If you have already taken out loans and are getting ready to graduate or have recently graduated, here are the key things to know.

KNOW WHAT YOU HAVE

First and foremost, find out before you leave school whether you have government or private loans, when the grace period ends (the brief time between graduation and work when you do not have to pay your loans back, usually six months), and make sure that your lender knows how to find you. That last step is really important. Oftentimes when you fill out your initial loan paperwork, you are using your parents' address or a school address. After you graduate, you want to make sure your lender knows where to find you. This will keep you from making the all-too-common mistake of missing your first repayments and becoming delinquent by accident.

COMMUNICATE

Next, if you find that you are having trouble paying back your loans, let your lender know immediately. This is one time you don't want to suffer in silence or get stuck in inaction. As awkward as it may feel, the earlier you can address this issue, the better off you will be. What kind of relief is available is dependent upon whether you have government loans or private loans. More relief is available, as of this writing, for government loans.

DEFERMENT, FORBEARANCE, FORGIVENESS, IBR, AND LOAN MODIFICATION

For federal loans, there are several types of relief available. There isn't a lot of wiggle room in the rules, but if you qualify it can make quite a difference. To take full advantage, you'll first want to make sure you understand exactly what kind of federal loans you have in the first place. If you do not know (and many people do not, so don't beat yourself up about this), visit *www.nslds.ed.gov* to find out.

To see if you qualify for any of the following five programs, contact your loan servicer directly (the organization to which you make your monthly loan payments).

▷ You will have to proactively ask your loan servicer about these options as none of these will be automatically offered to you. Your lender won't know you are in these situations if you don't tell them.

Loan Deferment

Under this type of loan relief, the repayment of your debt is suspended. If you have subsidized loans (direct or Stafford loans)

or Perkins loans, the interest will not accrue during a loan deferral. Essentially, it is as if your student loans are being temporarily put on ice. However, for all other types of federal loans, interest will continue to accrue, as it does under forbearance.

Example of situations that may qualify for a deferment include:

- You are going to school at least half time or are in a graduate fellowship program
- You are unemployed
- You are experiencing economic hardship
- You are serving in the Peace Corps or on active military duty

Loan Forbearance

In this type of loan relief, your monthly payments are either reduced or suspended for up to twelve months. During this temporary period you do not have to pay back any principal; *however,* the interest you owe continues to grow, or "accrue." The growing interest will get added back to your original debt. In other words, while you get some temporary relief, the amount you owe in total will grow during forbearance. There are two types of forbearance:

- **Discretionary:** Decision is up to your lender. It is based on qualifying situations of financial hardship or illness.
- **Mandatory:** Your lender *must* grant you forbearance. Qualifying circumstances include such reasons as: the total amount you owe each month is more than 20 percent of your income, you are in a medical or dental internship or residency, or you are in the National Guard and have been activated for duty.

Loan Forgiveness

As its name implies, loan forgiveness means that you are off the hook. If you qualify for this form of relief, some or all of your student loans are literally "forgiven," meaning you do not have to repay them. Because it's such a nice "deal," there are quite a few restrictions. Example of conditions where loan forgiveness may be an option:

- Specific types of volunteer work (e.g., AmeriCorps, Peace Corps, VISTA)
- Army National Guard participation
- Teaching or practicing medicine in specified low-income areas

▷ As of this writing, only direct federal loans are eligible for loan forgiveness. The rules are very detailed and it's important to review them considering your specific situation. For more information or an application, visit *www.loanconsolidation.ed.gov.*

Income-Based Repayment (IBR) Plans

Because student loan repayment has become burdensome for so many holders of government loans, a program call "IBR" or income-based repayment plans is currently available. In a nutshell, if you qualify for this program, the amount you have to repay is based on how much you are earning, rather than how much you owe. (Note: As of this writing, this plan is not open to PLUS loans made to parents or consolidation loans that include PLUS loans. PLUS loans are loans which are not based on financial need and are unsubsidized, meaning interest starts accruing from the get-go.)

How much you will pay under this plan is a factor of your income and family size. It is adjusted each year based on your current circumstances. Payments are made over a twenty-five year period and while they will increase with your income, they will never be more than they would be under a standard ten-year repayment plan. Other benefits of this program include loan forgiveness after twenty-five years of qualified participation. Also, if you are employed for ten years for a qualified public service organization and you make 120 on-time, in-full payments under an IBR plan, you might be eligible for loan forgiveness.

Private Loan Modification

If you have private loans at present, your options are not as plentiful. The key is to contact your lender to see if you can come to an agreement on a modified repayment plan—for instance, paying a lesser amount over a longer period of time—so as to avoid letting your debt go into default. With private loans, it is important to make sure you are in touch with your lender *before* you go into default. Once your lender sells your loan to a debt collector, it's out of their hands and you are in a much tougher position. As of this writing, it is very difficult to discharge private student loans even in an extreme situation such as bankruptcy. ■

Where to Go for More Information

Entire books have been written about student loans. We like Zac Bissonnette's *Debt-Free U* and The Princeton Review's *Paying For College Without Going Broke*. To get more information about your particular situation, here are our three favorite websites for comprehensive student loan overviews:

- *www.consumerfinance.gov/paying-for-college*
- *www.studentaid.ed.gov/types/loans*
- *www.studentloans.gov*

Student Loan Tips

Before you graduate make sure you know what kind of loans you have, when the grace period ends, and notify your lender of your new post-graduation address so you don't miss that first payment.

If you find yourself having trouble paying back your loans, notify your lender immediately. If you have federal loans your options may include deferment, forbearance, forgiveness, or an income-based repayment (IBR) plan. For private loans the options are narrower but it's worth talking to your lender to see if you can agree to a modified repayment plan.

If you are thinking about taking on student loans, remember our rough rule of thumb: Think long and hard about taking out more in total student loans than you think you will earn a year *on average* over the first ten years after graduation. This will help keep your loan payments from becoming too outsized relative to your income.

CHAPTER 12

Your Home

As Dorothy famously noted in *The Wizard of Oz*, "There's no place like home." There's something incredibly sweet about having a place that belongs just to you. Emotional attachments aside, the stark financial reality is that if you buy more house than you can comfortably afford, you will set yourself up for years of financial agony. The good news is that by the end of this chapter you will know how to prevent that mistake. Learning how to make the right decisions about whether, when, and what home to purchase will go a long way toward ensuring your financial security. This chapter provides several rules of thumb to help you address the critical issues surrounding home ownership:

- Deciding whether to rent or buy
- Figuring out how much house you can afford
- Doing the deal

Rent or Buy?

If approached prudently, buying a home can result in lasting emotional and financial benefits. However, as is the case with so many things in life, timing is everything with home ownership. This is particularly true when you're debating the question of whether to rent or buy.

You may have heard people equate renting to "throwing money down the drain." What these people probably didn't tell you is that you could end up throwing even *more* money down the drain if you make poor choices in buying a home. This brings us to our first rule of thumb for housing:

▷ Don't buy a house unless you plan to live in it for at least five years.

Isabelle's unfortunate experience with the real estate market helps explain why this is the case.

Isabelle thought she was making a smart move by jumping into the red-hot real estate market in Phoenix. She bought a home for $150,000 and expected to make a profit when she sold. Three years later, Isabelle was transferred to Kansas City. She put her home up for sale. Guess what? The housing market was in a funk. After six months of waiting—and paying for the mortgage on homes in both Phoenix and Kansas City at the same time—she finally got an offer for $135,000. Isabelle reluctantly took it.

If you buy a house that you plan to live in for less than five years, it is important to understand that what you are doing is essentially betting on the short-term direction of property prices. This kind of bet is an awful lot like gambling in Vegas. Things may go in your direction, but then again they may not.

Over the long run, housing prices have gone up. However, you typically need at least five years to have reasonably high odds that your home will appreciate enough in price to offset the additional costs of home ownership. With a mere three years under her belt, Isabelle cried into her martini when she realized just how much her foray into home ownership had cost her. Isabelle's situation could have been worse had she not followed our next important rule of thumb:

▷ Don't buy a house until you have enough money for a 20 percent down payment.

As a result of having made a 20 percent down payment, there was somewhat of a silver lining for Isabelle. Even though she sold her house for $15,000 less than her original purchase price, she received enough money from the sale (after the realtor's cut) to pay off her remaining outstanding mortgage loan. By contrast, if Isabelle had purchased her home with only a 5 percent down payment, she would have had to come up with *another* $11,000 to pay off her mortgage loan.

The Dangers of Buying a House with Less than 20 Percent Down

A 5 percent down payment on a $150,000 house is $7,500. If Isabelle had chosen to buy her house with just 5 percent down, she would have had to borrow the remaining $142,500 from the bank. After three years of mortgage payments, she would have $138,000 remaining on her loan. (The way mortgages work: in the early years most of your monthly payment goes to interest, instead of to paying down the principal, which is the amount you actually borrowed.) However, she'd only pocket $127,000 from the sale of her home ($135,000 sale price minus $8,000 for the real estate agent's commission). That means Isabelle would have had to come up with *another* $11,000 to pay off her mortgage loan. Ouch.

When you buy a home, you also need to be sure that you can afford to pay for the cost of owning that home. This brings us to our third rule of thumb:

▷ Don't buy a house unless you understand—and can pay for—the three additional costs of home ownership.

The Three Additional Costs of Home Ownership

- **Closing costs:** These are costs to transfer a home into your name at the time of purchase. They typically run 2 to 4 percent of the purchase price of a home.
- **Selling costs:** Unless you sell your home yourself, you'll need to pay a real estate agent. Realtors typically charge a fee of 5 to 6 percent of the sale price of your home for their services.
- **Cost of maintaining your home:** These costs will typically run around 3 percent of the purchase price of your home per year. They include property taxes (1 to 2 percent), homeowner's insurance (0.5 to 1.0 percent), and general maintenance/upkeep (1 percent and up).

Finally, you may be asking, "But what about the tax break? I've heard that home ownership is the ultimate tax break." Home ownership can indeed provide nice tax benefits. However, the tax benefits are not automatic.

UNDERSTANDING WHAT IT MEANS TO "DEDUCT YOUR MORTGAGE"

Because a house is such a major purchase, most people have to take out a home loan (called a mortgage) to get enough money to pay the seller for the house. When you calculate your taxes, the government allows you to deduct a portion of the interest that you pay on that mortgage. Unfortunately, the benefits of this tax deduction often get overblown, as this deduction is not automatic. You must itemize your tax deductions to receive it. Additionally, even if you can take this deduction, you don't get a dollar-for-dollar reduction in your taxes. For example, if your marginal tax rate is 25 percent, the mortgage interest tax break saves you $25 for every $100 in interest you pay. In other words, you still pay the remaining $75 of interest out of your own pocket. We talk more about taxes in **CHAPTER 14**.

How Much House Can You Afford?

One of the dirty little secrets of home ownership is how many people are "house poor"—as a result of buying more house than they could afford. Now, like a bottomless pit, the associated house payments and expenses are sucking them down into financial distress. So how do you avoid becoming house poor? You follow our fourth rule of thumb:

▷ Aim for your housing-related expenses to total no more than 25 percent of your gross income.

When we say housing-related expenses, we mean your mortgage payment, property taxes, insurance, maintenance, and upkeep. What's the rationale for this rule of thumb? It all goes back to the Power Trio of Budgeting from **CHAPTER 5**. Recall that we recommend that roughly 45 percent of your gross income go toward foundation expenses, including your housing-related expenses.

If your housing-related expenses exceed 25 percent of your gross income, that won't leave you with much wiggle room for your other foundation expenses (such as your transportation, basic groceries, medical, debt repayment, and child care). It may also force you to dip into your fun and future funds, which as you learned in **CHAPTER 5** is not a financially savvy move if you can help it.

In the following table we show approximately how much house you can buy given your income level at varying levels of interest rates.

How Much House Can You Comfortably Afford?*

Your Income	Interest Rate on Your Mortgage				
	4%	5%	6%	7%	8%
$20,000	$87,000	$78,000	$69,000	$63,000	$57,000
$30,000	$131,000	$116,000	$104,000	$94,000	$85,000
$40,000	$175,000	$155,000	$139,000	$125,000	$114,000
$50,000	$218,000	$194,000	$174,000	$157,000	$142,000
$60,000	$262,000	$233,000	$208,000	$188,000	$170,000
$70,000	$305,000	$272,000	$243,000	$219,000	$199,000
$80,000	$349,000	$310,000	$278,000	$251,000	$227,000
$90,000	$393,000	$349,000	$313,000	$282,000	$256,000
$100,000	$436,000	$388,000	$347,000	$313,000	$284,000

*Assumes a 20 percent down payment, a thirty-year fixed-rate mortgage, and that your monthly mortgage payment is 20 percent of your gross income (so you have room for other housing-related costs). Total home price figures are rounded to the nearest $1,000.

As you look over this table, there are a couple of things to keep in mind. First, the primary driver of how much house you can afford is the size of your monthly mortgage payment. The size of your monthly mortgage payment, in turn, is dramatically influenced by the interest rate you are charged on your mortgage loan. That interest rate will be a function of the economic environment at the time you purchase your home as well as your credit score. The higher your credit score, the lower your interest rate. You can get a sense for the kind of interest rate you will be charged by getting your current credit score at *www.myfico.com*. This brings us to our fifth rule of thumb:

▷ It is very important to figure out how much house
  you can afford *before* you go house shopping.

We strongly urge you to tell your realtor *not* to show you homes with asking prices higher than your maximum number. That's the easiest way to avoid the temptation to "stretch" for more house than you can afford.

Doing the Deal

Once you commit to staying in one place for five years, have 20 percent for a down payment, understand the associated costs of home ownership, and figure out how much you can afford to spend on the total purchase price of a home, you are ready to start "doing the deal."

STEP #1

GET PRE-APPROVED

The first step is to go get pre-approved for a mortgage. You can do this directly with a lender or through a mortgage broker. When we say "lender," we mean a financial institution such as a bank and/ or specialty financial firm that focuses on mortgage lending. By contrast, a mortgage broker is someone who acts as the go-between among you and various lenders. The benefit of using a mortgage broker is that with one stop you can get quotes from various lenders. However, you can sometimes find better rates if you are willing to do the legwork yourself.

Getting pre-approved shows realtors and prospective sellers that you are really serious. You do not, however, have to get your final mortgage from the lender that pre-approves you. You are welcome to shop around for a better interest rate. When you do shop around for your final mortgage, remember to try to keep your shopping within a two-week period so that it will count as one inquiry on your credit report. This helps protect your credit score. If you have trouble getting pre-approved, this step will let you know about any financial troubles you need to address before you start the house-shopping process.

Buyer Beware: You May "Qualify" for More House than You Can Afford

A lender may tell you that you qualify or are approved for a larger mortgage than you can afford—that is, a mortgage that would result in your monthly housing costs being significantly greater than 25 percent of your gross income. Bear in mind, however, that lenders are in the business of lending money. Therefore, it makes sense that they would offer you as much as they feel they prudently can. To be blunt, the lender doesn't care if you can't afford to retire, take vacations, or send your kids to college. As long as you repay their loan, they are happy. Please do not fall into the all-too-common trap of buying a more expensive house just because you qualify for a bigger mortgage. That is a recipe for extreme financial stress.

STEP #2

MAKE SURE YOU HAVE SAVED ENOUGH TO PAY 20 PERCENT OF THE PURCHASE PRICE AS AN INITIAL DOWN PAYMENT

You can buy a house for less than 20 percent down. However, if you choose to do that, mortgage lenders will require you to buy something called private mortgage insurance, commonly abbreviated as PMI. What this means is that lenders are sufficiently concerned about your ability to repay your loan that they make *you* pay for the insurance to make sure they get paid back in the event that you can't make your loan payments. Putting 20 percent down gives you a nice buffer if you unexpectedly have to sell your home during a market slump (recall Isabelle's experience). It also means your monthly mortgage payments will be less than they would be with a smaller down payment.

STEP #3

CHOOSE THE *RIGHT* MORTGAGE

There are about as many variations on mortgages as there are flavors of ice cream. We have a keep-it-simple recommendation for you:

▷ Go with a thirty-year fixed-rate mortgage.

With this kind of loan, you make a fixed monthly payment until you finally pay off your entire loan at the end of year thirty. You can also get fixed-rate mortgages for shorter time periods. The fifteen-year fixed-rate mortgage is the most common of the shorter loans. With a shorter loan, you will have higher monthly payments but lower total interest costs over the life of the loan.

Note that some lenders now offer forty-year or even fifty-year fixed-rate loans. We urge you not to consider anything longer than a thirty-year fixed-rate loan as otherwise you'll end up paying way too much in total interest costs.

What about Hybrid Adjustable-Rate Mortgages (ARMs), Interest-Only, and Other "Exotic" Mortgages?

With a hybrid ARM, your monthly payments are fixed for a specified number of years and then vary after that. After the fixed period, the interest rate on this type of mortgage typically changes annually, which means the amount of your monthly mortgage payment also changes every year. These loans are generally structured so that you pay off your entire loan over a thirty-year period. If you are sure you'll live in your house for no longer than five to ten years, then this type of mortgage could make sense for you. The initial interest rate and mortgage payments are often lower than with a pure fixed-rate mortgage. However, if you end up staying in your house longer than expected (as many people do), *your interest payments could very well spike*. In this situation, your ARM will end up becoming very dangerous to your financial health.

We *strongly* urge you to stay away from interest-only mortgages. When you are paying interest only, that means every last penny of what you pay in your monthly mortgage payment goes to interest. *None* of it goes toward paying down your loan. Think about that. You are borrowing money to buy a house, and yet you aren't paying back any of the loan.

We also strongly urge you to stay away from other exotic mortgages, such as option ARMs. If you get an exotic mortgage and fall on hard times, you could very well lose your home.

STEP #4

START HOUSE HUNTING

Your primary goal in this step will be to find a house you love that doesn't cause you to blow your budget.

If you follow the rules of thumb we've discussed in this chapter, home ownership can be a really beautiful thing. While it takes some time, you *will* one day own your home outright if you consistently make your monthly payments, and you'll no longer have a monthly mortgage payment. ■

How to Think about Home Ownership

The keys to your "rent or buy" decision are your answers to the following questions:

Will you stay put for at least five years? Can you afford a 20 percent down payment? Do you understand the three additional costs of home ownership? If the answer to all three is yes, you are ready to buy from a financial standpoint.

Your goal is to make sure your foundation costs do not exceed 45 percent of your gross income.

Typically, that means keeping your total housing-related expenses to no more than 25 percent of your gross income.

When it comes to mortgages, our keep-it-simple recommendation is to go with a thirty-year fixed-rate mortgage.

Please don't even think about an interest-only mortgage. If that's the only way to afford the house you want, unfortunately that means the house is out of your price range.

CHAPTER 13

Your Car

After a home, the second-largest purchase most people make is a car. While homes and cars are very different items, they do have one big thing in common. As with your home, if you buy a more expensive car than you can afford, you are putting your financial security at risk. You could have difficulty saving for your future and could also quite possibly set yourself up to struggle just to make ends meet. The good news is that if you are prudent about your car purchase, you will be taking an important step toward ensuring your financial success.

In this chapter, we're going talk about the key aspects of buying a car:

- How much can you afford to spend on a car?
- New or used? Buy or lease?
- Doing the deal

How Much Car Can You Afford?

It's human nature to want to treat yourself to a fancy new car. However, if you buy more car than you can afford, that dream car can quickly turn into a financial nightmare—as it did for Mandy.

Mandy was absolutely thrilled when she was offered her dream job at a top-notch public relations firm. She decided to celebrate by buying a car that projected the right image for her new position. Mandy noticed there were many luxury SUVs in her company's parking garage. When she drove off the dealer's lot with a similar new car, she thought she had arrived. After living with her car payment for a few months, however, she realized that her stylish wheels came with some serious strings attached. Her hefty monthly payment and associated car costs were a huge drain on her finances. Despite her big new salary, Mandy felt like she was struggling financially just to make ends meet.

A car is a very significant purchase. If you are like most people, you'll have to take out a car loan. In addition to the purchase price, your total cost of car ownership will include gas, insurance, parking, tolls, and maintenance. So how much can you afford to spend on a car? Our advice is . . .

▷ Aim to keep your total car-related expenses to 10 percent or *less* of your total gross income.

The logic around how much car you can afford is very similar to the logic we used to recommend how much house you can afford. In other words, how much car you can afford is driven first and foremost by a desire to keep your spending in line with our Power Trio of Budgeting (discussed in **CHAPTER 5**) so you can both enjoy today and save for the future.

In the following chart, we show roughly how much you could afford to pay for a car at varying levels of income. For example, suppose your annual income is $50,000 and your credit score qualifies you for an 8 percent interest rate on a car loan. (See **CHAPTER 3** for a refresher on credit scores.) If you want to keep your life devoid of financial angst, you should buy a car with a total purchase price (including tax, title, and license) of no more than $18,000.

How Much Car Can You Comfortably Afford?*

Your Income	Interest Rate on Your Five-Year Car Loan				
	5%	6%	7%	8%	9%
$20,000	$7,700	$7,500	$7,400	$7,200	$7,000
$30,000	$11,600	$11,300	$11,000	$10,800	$10,500
$40,000	$15,500	$15,100	$14,700	$14,400	$14,100
$50,000	$19,300	$18,900	$18,400	$18,000	$17,600
$60,000	$23,200	$22,600	$22,100	$21,600	$21,100
$70,000	$27,000	$26,400	$25,800	$25,200	$24,600
$80,000	$30,900	$30,200	$29,500	$28,800	$28,100
$90,000	$34,800	$33,900	$33,100	$32,400	$31,600
$100,000	$38,600	$37,700	$36,800	$36,000	$35,100

*Assumes a 20 percent down payment, a five-year car loan, and that your monthly car payment is 7 percent of your gross income (so you have room for other transportation-related costs). Total car price figures are rounded to the nearest $100.

This chart assumes that you pay 20 percent of the purchase price of the car upfront as a down payment, take out a car loan of no longer than five years (shorter is better!), and that your monthly car payment is 7 percent of your gross income. We assume the additional costs of car ownership (such as insurance, gas, parking, tolls, and maintenance) equal 3 percent of your gross income, thus bringing your total car-related expenses to 10 percent of your gross income. Note that these additional costs of car ownership are just an estimate. To get a more precise figure, you can calculate the actual numbers for your personal situation. We highly recommend you go through this exercise *before* you consider purchasing a car so you have a fuller picture of how much your car of choice will really cost you.

If the figures in this chart seem low to you, you have now discovered why Mandy found herself struggling financially when she was merely "doing what everyone else was." Millions of people have made the financial mistake of buying more car than they can afford.

New or Used? Buy or Lease?

Two key considerations when buying your car are the following: Should you get a new or used car? If you choose a new car, is it smarter to buy the car outright or lease? Let's talk about these decisions.

Deciding between a new and a used car is a highly personal decision. The tradeoffs you make with your money are very specific to your values and priorities. At the same time, if you decide to buy a new car, we want to make sure you are aware of the following fact:

▷ The minute you drive a new car off the dealership lot, it starts losing value.

A typical car loses almost 50 percent of its value over the first three years.

While the value of a home typically goes up over time, the value of a car only goes down. The technical term for this unpleasant phenomenon is "depreciation," and the severity with which it happens varies from one type of car to the next. If you buy a brand-new car every couple of years in order to always have the latest hot car, you will be throwing a lot of money down the drain in lost depreciation. This doesn't mean a brand-new car is bad—it just means that buying one makes the most financial sense when you plan on keeping it for a long time. What this also means is that a used car can be a very compelling value. If you buy a two- or three-year-old used car (frequently referred to as "previously owned"), you could save almost half of the purchase price as compared to buying that same car brand new. The key to protecting yourself is to buy that used car from a trusted, reliable source.

How much you spend on your car will ultimately be a personal decision. Our goal is simply to make sure you are fully aware of the financial tradeoff embedded in your decision. If you opt for a new car, you'll need to decide whether you want to buy or lease that car. Here's our view:

▷ When it comes to leasing, we strongly urge you to pass.

While leasing often sounds like a good deal on the surface, it's typically not nearly as good a deal as buying a car outright. First, if you buy a car with 20 percent down and a five-year loan, guess what happens at the start of year six? You no longer have car payments. You can take the money you used to put toward car payments and allocate it to fun or future expenses. By contrast, with a lease, you never stop having car payments because you're never putting money into buying a car. At the end of the lease period, you're done paying, but you still don't own a car. Additionally, during the lease period, you are subject to mileage limits. Say you end up moving and having to commute farther than you expected—you could blow your mileage allotment before the lease is up and have to pay hefty fees. Finally, we also don't like the fact that when you lease, you become "locked in." What happens if you get offered your dream job in New York City, where you no longer need a car? If you break your lease, there will be stiff financial penalties to pay.

Holly walked in the front door of a dealership knowing that she wanted to keep her total car-related costs to less than 10 percent of her gross income. The salesperson said, "No problem. I can give you that monthly payment *and* a better car. All you have to do is lease, not buy." Holly signed on the dotted line and drove off with a snazzy two-seat convertible. A few months later, she became pregnant with twins and needed a bigger car. Unfortunately, she still had over two years left on her three-year lease. When the car dealer told her it would cost several thousand dollars to break her lease, she almost lost her lunch.

Doing the Deal

Until the Internet became mainstream, you had only one option when it came to buying a car. You ate your Wheaties, braced yourself for a high-pressure sales pitch, and headed off to a car dealership to see if you could make it through the day without getting royally squeezed. These days, things are very different. Thanks to the Internet, the process of researching and buying a car can actually be pleasant—or at least less stressful! These days you can buy your car through the "Internet door" at a car dealership. Unless you just love to negotiate, the Internet door is the one we urge you to walk through to buy your car.

Here's our recommended car-buying action plan:

1. **Decide how much car you can afford, and make sure you can put 20 percent of the purchase price down.** (Note: The money for that 20 percent down payment can come from savings and/or from the money you receive for trading in your existing car.) The precise amount of car that you can afford is a function not just of your income but also of the interest rate you will be charged on your car loan. To see what kind of rate you can expect given your current credit score, check out *www.myfico.com*.

   Note: Don't forget you can often get more car for your money by considering a two- or three-year-old used car.

2. **Decide what make and model of car you want to buy.** A great way to start this process is to do some online research. You can easily compare the different cars in your price range at websites such as *www.edmunds.com*, *www.kbb.com* (Kelley Blue Book), *www.consumerreports.org* (where you should go to the "Cars" tab; note a paid subscription is required for this particular site), and *www.fueleconomy.gov*.

   Note: If you decide to buy a used car, before you sign on the dotted line, be sure to go to www.carfax.com *and check the car's history using its vehicle identification number, or VIN. This will enable you to make sure the used car you are considering doesn't have a dicey past—that it wasn't in a flood or hasn't had an extensive repair history.*

3. **Price your car.** There are a number of websites that offer free car-pricing services. The way these sites work is that they pass along your inquiry to local area car dealers, who will e-mail or call you with their no-haggle price. Websites that provide this service for both new and used cars include *www.autobytel.com*, *www.carsdirect.com*, *www.cars.com*, and *www.pricequote.com*.

Note: Get at least two quotes. If you are looking for a used car, we also recommend checking out www.carmax.com *and local dealerships that offer manufacturer-certified preowned cars.*

How do I know I'm getting a good price for my car?

To find out how much a dealer paid for your car of choice, you can go to websites such as *www.edmunds.com* and *www.kbb.com* to look up the dealer invoice. It will depend on your car model of choice, but generally we think paying anywhere from 2 to 4 percent over dealer invoice constitutes a fair deal.

---

4. **Comparison shop for your auto loan.** *Always* shop around for your car loan *before* buying your car at the car dealership. The reason is that the car dealership is not the only place you can take out a car loan. You can go to a bank or a finance company that specializes in car loans. Car dealerships make a lot of money on these loans, so you will likely be encouraged to use their "convenient in-house financing." Be forewarned that the dealer may charge you a higher interest rate than your local bank or a specialty finance company for your car loan. Lining up other financing alternatives *before* you go to the dealership is the best way to protect yourself.

Note: Get at least two quotes for your car loan. Start at your bank and also check Web-based lenders such as www.capitaloneauto finance.com, www.pnc.com, *and* www.eloan.com. *As with mortgages, be sure to do this car-loan shopping within a two-week period to protect your credit score. Additionally, before signing your final paperwork, be sure to read the fine print. For instance, if you're taking out a loan directly from the dealership, you'll want to make sure the interest rate you thought you were getting is the one to which you are contractually agreeing. Attractive offers for 0 percent financing are typically only for qualified buyers, so check the actual interest rate stated in the paperwork.*

5. **Once at the dealership, stand firm.** If you contact the dealer through their Internet sales department, you typically will not be pushed to consider another, more expensive car. However, it's human nature to get tempted to look around. It's also easy to get suckered into last-minute add-ons. We urge you to stand firm to your budget.

   Note: Extended warranties are extremely *profitable for car dealerships, so expect to get a good push to buy one. We are not fans. Generally, you are better off taking the money you would have paid toward that warranty and saving it on your own.*

If you follow this game plan, you'll be in great shape for your car buying. Don't be afraid to ask questions when you are at the dealership. Make sure you understand all the paperwork. This paperwork can be confusing for even the most seasoned car buyer. If there's anything that doesn't make sense to you, don't sign for your car until you get it clarified. ■

Drive Safe, Buy Smart

Generally speaking, aim for your total car-related expenses to be no more than 10 percent of your total gross income. The exact amount you can afford to spend, however, will depend on where you stand in the Power Trio of Budgeting (as we discussed in **CHAPTER 5**).

If you need a car loan, we recommend a down payment of at least 20 percent and a loan of no longer than five years.

To avoid the pain of car-dealership negotiations, follow our easy car-buying process. If you are interested in learning more about any of the steps, the websites *www.edmunds.com* and *www.kbb.com* have a number of useful articles.

CHAPTER 14

Your Income Taxes

We're not going to try to convince you that there is anything fun about taxes. As far as we can tell, there isn't. However, there's no escaping them. Taxes consume roughly 25 percent of the average working person's earnings. That's quite a bite. (That figure can be even higher if you earn an above-average income or if you live in a state with above-average tax rates.) As such, we think it's important for everyone to know the basics about where those taxes are going. This chapter will address:

- The types of taxes owed on your income
- When you should pay your taxes
- How to file your tax return

Types of Taxes Owed on Your Income

Generally speaking, everyone who earns income is required to pay federal taxes to the U.S. government. This income can come from various sources, including your work, your investments, or even gambling winnings. In addition, you may have to pay taxes to state and local governments, depending upon the state and city of your work and residence.

FEDERAL TAXES

There are three different components to the taxes levied on your income at a national level.

Federal Income Tax

The amount of tax you are required to pay depends upon your taxable income and on your tax filing status. For instance, single filers pay different tax rates than married couples filing jointly.

Your taxable income is your total income less exemptions and allowable deductions. Exemptions and deductions are government-prescribed reductions to your total income that lower the amount of taxes you pay. You get to take an exemption for yourself and for any dependents in your household. In 2013, each personal exemption reduces your taxable income by $3,900. We'll talk more about allowable deductions in the last section of the chapter.

The following tax rate schedule shows the rates at which different levels of taxable income are taxed for calendar year 2013. This schedule is published and updated annually to adjust for inflation by the Internal Revenue Service (IRS). You'll notice that not every dollar you earn is taxed at the same rate. This is called a progressive tax system, where the tax rate increases as your taxable income goes up.

▷ The rate at which your very last dollar of income is taxed is what's known as your marginal tax rate.

	Your Tax Filing Status			
Tax Rate	Single Filer (not married)	Head of Household (single parent)	Married/Filing Separately (to keep your finances separate)	Married/ Filing Jointly or Qualifying Widow(er)
10%	Up to $8,925	Up to $12,750	Up to $8,925	Up to $17,850
15%	$8,926 to $36,250	$12,751 to $48,600	$8,926 to $36,250	$17,851 to $72,500
25%	$36,251 to $87,850	$48,601 to $125,450	$36,251 to $73,200	$72,501 to $146,400
28%	$87,851 to $183,250	$125,451 to $203,150	$73,201 to $111,525	$146,401 to $223,050
33%	$183,251 to $393,350	$203,151 to $398,350	$111,526 to $199,175	$223,051 to $398,350
35%	$393,351 to $400,000	$398,351 to $425,000	$199,176 to $225,000	$398,351 to $450,000
39.6%	$400,001 or more	$425,001 or more	$225,001 or more	$450,001 or more

Source: *www.irs.gov*

An easy way to estimate your federal income tax for the current year is to use a tax calculator on a website such as *www.dinkytown .net*.

Social Security Tax

This tax is levied only on income you earn from working. It is not levied on any other income, such as that from investments or gambling. The money collected is intended to provide you with monthly benefits in your old age. If you work as an employee for someone else, you pay 6.2 percent of your salary, and your employer also pays Uncle Sam an amount equal to 6.2 percent of your salary. If you are self-employed, you must pay the entire 12.4 percent yourself. This tax applies up to a salary limit of $113,700 in 2013. Earnings in excess of this amount are not subject to Social Security tax.

Medicare Tax

As with Social Security, this tax is levied only on income earned from working. It is intended to provide medical benefits in your old age. The current Medicare tax rate is 1.45 percent and applies to all your income from working, with no salary limit. Again, employers are required to match this amount. If you are self-employed, you must pay the entire 2.9 percent yourself.

STATE AND LOCAL TAXES

Many state governments, and some local ones, also impose income tax. The amount of tax you pay depends on the state and city you work and live in. Most people who live in the forty-three states that have income taxes typically end up being taxed in a range of 3 to 6 percent on an effective basis; but marginal rates can go into the double digits for high-income earners in a high-tax state like California. The seven states that do not currently levy state income taxes are Alaska, Florida, Nevada, South Dakota, Texas, Washington, and Wyoming.

▷ When you add up what you pay in *all* of the above taxes and divide that sum by your total (before-tax) salary, you end up with your effective, or total, tax rate.

In other words, you find out effectively what you paid in total taxes on your income. The effective tax rate for most people is, on average, around 25 percent of their salary.

When Do You Pay Your Taxes?

In the United States, we have a "pay-as-you-go" tax system. In other words, we are required to pay taxes at the time we earn income. If you work as an employee of someone else, estimated taxes are taken out before you receive your paycheck. The amount of income tax deducted is based on your salary level and the number of exemptions you claimed on the W-4 form you filled out on your first day of work. As such, it is important to claim the appropriate number of exemptions so that the total amount of income tax withheld for the calendar year will approximate your expected total taxes for the year. (Instructions are included on the W-4 form.) This will help you avoid the unpleasant surprise at tax time of having to pay an additional amount beyond what was withheld from your paycheck by your employer. (Note that Social Security and Medicare taxes are also taken out each pay period, and the amount is based on your salary.)

For those of you who are self-employed, you must pay one quarter of your total estimated taxes for the current tax year in April, June, September, and the following January in order to meet the pay-as-you-go requirement of our tax system. More details on this obligation can be found at *www.irs.gov.*

How to File Your Taxes

All taxpayers are required to submit final tax returns (or a request for an extension of time to file your tax return) to federal and state/local tax authorities by April 15 of each year for the prior calendar year.

▷ April 15 is Tax Day.

Tax returns are the documents that enable you to formally settle up with the government each year. If the final total tax amount shown on these documents is less than the total periodic payments you made during the year, you will get a tax refund. If, however, the total tax amount on your final tax return is more than your periodic payments, you must pay the balance due by April 15. While many people view a tax refund as a gift, it's actually just a return of your own money.

You have three basic options for doing your taxes:

1. Have someone do it for you. You may go either to a tax preparation firm (such as H&R Block or Jackson Hewitt) or to your local certified public accountant (CPA).
2. Do-it-yourself using online tax preparation software such as TurboTax or TaxCut.
3. Do-it-yourself the old-fashioned way by filling out the tax forms manually. The necessary forms can be obtained at the post office or from the IRS website (*www.irs.gov*).

Unless you just love doing your taxes, we recommend the first option. But before you sit down with the tax preparer, there are a few topics with which you should be familiar.

ITEMIZED VERSUS STANDARD DEDUCTIONS

One of the most common questions about taxes is "Can I deduct this?" People love tax deductions and for good reason. Deductions reduce your tax bill. The most common available deductions are student loan interest, mortgage interest, charitable contributions, property tax, state/local income taxes, and medical and nonreimbursed job-related expenses that exceed a specified percentage of your income.

However, there are two key things about deductions that are important to note:

● **You can only deduct the aforementioned items if you itemize your deductions.** The government offers people a choice of taking the greater of either a standard deduction or an itemized deduction. A "standard" deduction is a set amount that the government allows each person to deduct from their taxable income to help lower their taxes. The precise dollar figure is based on your tax filing status. For example, in 2013 the standard deduction was $6,100 for single filers and $12,200 for married joint filers. If after adding up all of your qualifying deductions, such as mortgage interest, charitable contributions, and nonfederal taxes, you find that they are greater than the standard deduction, the government allows you to itemize your deductions and get a bigger tax benefit. We highlight this point because many people think their mortgage interest is an automatic tax deduction. You do not get *any* deduction on your mortgage interest unless you itemize your deductions. Interestingly, in any given year, roughly two-thirds of tax filers wind up using the standard deduction. Be sure to talk to your tax preparer about whether you should take the standard deduction or the itemized deduction.

● **A deduction does *not* reduce your tax bill dollar for dollar.** A $1,000 deduction does not reduce your total tax bill by $1,000. Rather, your tax bill is reduced by the amount of your deduction times your marginal tax rate. Recall, this is the federal tax rate at which your "last dollar" of income is taxed. For example, if you have $1,000 in mortgage interest that you list as an itemized deduction and your marginal tax rate is 25 percent, you save $250.

TAX CREDITS

Tax credits are even more valuable than deductions. The reason is that a tax credit is a dollar-for-dollar reduction in your overall tax bill. If you get a $1,000 tax credit, your overall tax bill is reduced by $1,000. However, many tax credits are subject to income limits, which vary from credit to credit. If you make too much money, you can't take certain credits. The most common kinds of tax credits include earned income tax credits, child or dependent care tax credits, education tax credits, and energy tax credits. If you use a tax preparer, be sure to ask that person if you qualify for any tax credits.

SUPPORTING DOCUMENTATION

Collect the following documents before you go on your visit to the tax preparer:

● **Form W-2:** This is the year-end form that summarizes what you were paid and how much was already sent to the government in withholding. Your employer must provide you with your Form W-2 by January 31 of the following year.

- **Form 1099:** Your bank and/or brokerage firm will send you this form by January 31. Form 1099 summarizes any interest and dividends received on your taxable investments. If you did any work as an independent contractor, your income would be reported on this form.

- **Additional information:** If you plan to itemize your deductions, you'll need all receipts and any other documentation supporting the deductions you claim. If you are self-employed, you will need the documents supporting your business revenues and expenses.

With this information, the tax preparer will be able to complete your final tax return. If you are interested, in **APPENDIX C** we list the most common tax forms required by the IRS. ∎

Tax-Related Documents to Save

Save copies of your final tax returns for all eternity as your tax returns may prove useful down the line, such as if there is ever a question about how much Social Security to which you are entitled. Save all materials used to create your final tax return (W-2s, 1099s, and documents supporting all deductions) for at least six years. If you are ever audited by the IRS, you'll need this paperwork to prove the accuracy of your tax return.

Be Smart about Your Taxes

For most people, combined federal, state, and local income taxes eat up approximately 25 percent of their pay.

To minimize the pain of doing your taxes and to reduce the risk of errors, we recommend either paying a tax professional to do your taxes (such as H&R Block, Jackson Hewitt, or your local CPA) or using tax preparation software (such as TurboTax or TaxCut).

Talk to your tax preparer about whether you should take the standard or the itemized deduction. Also ask if you are eligible for any tax credits.

CHAPTER 15

Your Heart and Your Money

When coupling up, most people think to talk about their feelings and priorities when it comes to topics such as religion or having children. Unfortunately, all too many couples neglect to talk frankly about money. If you and your significant other are not on the same page financially speaking, that's an invitation for arguments. Disagreements over money consistently top the list of issues with which typical couples grapple. Thankfully, there are a few simple steps that you can take to ensure your financial success and keep money-related disputes with your partner to a minimum. Remember, the vast majority of people do not do a good job of managing their personal finances. Thus, as you welcome someone into your life, you'll want to make sure you both see eye to eye about how to stay financially healthy.

This chapter is written in the context of your being in a committed relationship. However, even if you are not in a relationship right now, please keep reading—you never know when you'll turn the corner and run smack into "the one." If you'd like to read even more on this subject, we recommend our second book, *Get Financially Naked: How to Talk Money with Your Honey.*

In this chapter, we'll talk about these issues:

- Revealing yourself—financially speaking
- Creating a mutually agreed-upon financial game plan
- Protecting yourself—because unfortunately love doesn't always last forever

Revealing Yourself—Financially Speaking

Garth was everything Gretchen had ever wanted in a man. He was constantly showering her with thoughtful gifts, big and small. He had a shiny new sports car. When he popped the question with a huge ring, Gretchen thought her dreams had come true. After the wedding, however, the phone calls started. Nope, not from another woman—from collection agencies! Turned out the gifts, the car, the ring, even the wedding and honeymoon, were all paid for with plastic. Gretchen hadn't wanted to bring up money matters before they were married because she didn't want to seem like a gold digger and scare Garth away. Now she was a newlywed descending into bankruptcy.

A survey commissioned by *Money* magazine discovered that a shockingly high percentage of couples did not know, or incorrectly assumed, what their partner's financial priorities were.

▷ Financial compatibility is every bit as important to the success of a relationship as emotional and physical compatibility.

Being honest with each other upfront about the good, the bad, and the ugly of your financial situation and your financial values is an excellent investment in your relationship. Once your relationship is at a stage where you are contemplating being with your partner for the long term, revealing yourself (financially speaking) is a critical step. We realize it may be an awkward topic to broach. But once you do it, what you need to do in terms of actions is actually pretty straightforward.

▷ Exchange a list of what you own (the big things), a list of what you owe, and your most recent credit reports. If this feels like too much at once, consider having a series of financial date nights where you gradually share this information.

Each of these three pieces of information provides important insight that will enable you to get a more complete understanding of each other's financial situation. As clinical as it may sound, this step is the foundation for your financial partnership. This information enables you to have the building blocks to figure out what you two need to do to create your desired mutual financial future. It's also a very good idea to talk about how money was discussed (or not discussed) when you were growing up. This type of open conversation can go a long way toward enabling each person in the relationship to understand where the other is coming from. Additionally, going through this process may help protect you from being hurt by someone else's financial negligence.

Create a Game Plan

Once you've shared your financial histories, it's time to set up a financial game plan for the two of you. This is going to include making a few simple decisions. Will you have joint or separate bank accounts? Who will handle which financial chores? How often will you do a joint financial checkup?

JOINT OR SEPARATE BANK ACCOUNTS?

This is a highly personal decision. You have two basic options, and here's how to think about them:

- **Option A:** Some couples prefer to be united in every possible way, including financially. If you opt for joint accounts, we recommend that you set a dollar amount above which you both agree to consult each other before spending. In addition, you may want to consider setting an amount of money you each are allowed to spend every month with no questions asked. When couples fight about money, often it is because one felt the other spent money he or she should not have.

- **Option B:** Other couples like to do the financial three-way—yours, mine, and ours. The "ours" account is typically a shared one for household/joint expenses. If you take this approach, be very clear with each other about what does and does not constitute a joint expense.

WHO HANDLES WHICH FINANCIAL CHORES?

Here you'll need to decide who handles routine bill paying, household budgeting, and saving/investment decisions. In some households one person does all three, while in other households the tasks are divided up. There are two keys to ensuring that financial chores are handled appropriately. The first is to be clear with each other about who is responsible for what so nothing falls through the cracks. The second is to commit to keeping each other informed about the state of your mutual finances. For instance, if one partner is in charge of investments and an investment goes south, it is important to make sure the other is aware of this fact. Likewise, if one partner is in charge of budgeting and household expenses soar in a particular area, this is information that needs to be discussed.

FREQUENCY OF FINANCIAL CHECKUPS

We *strongly* recommend that you commit to at least an annual household financial checkup. By this we mean that once a year, you sit down together and literally tally up what you own, what you owe, and you review each other's credit reports. During this review, talk about whether there are any adjustments you want to make to your budget, whether you are meeting your savings goals, and whether you are both still comfortable with how your money is invested. Your annual financial checkup forces you to get financially "naked" with each other. This is an important step toward making sure that your joint finances are moving in the right direction. (As a side note, recall from **CHAPTER 3** that reviewing your credit reports each year helps you spot any fraudulent or unusual activity that shouldn't be on your reports.)

If one person is responsible for all financial chores, this annual financial checkup is even more critical. The reason is that it can be very easy for the other partner to mentally check out on the household finances—which in turn can lead to all sorts of troubles. Just imagine a woman who lets her husband handle all the money, only to find out he's spent all their retirement accounts *and* drained all their home equity to prop up his business. Unfortunately, stuff like this happens all too frequently.

Your annual financial checkup is also a great time to make sure both of you know where all your important papers and accounts are stored. You'll both want to know at which bank or financial institution you have your checking, savings, and retirement accounts. You'll also want to make sure you both know where your insurance policies, deeds and titles to homes and cars, and wills are kept.

Protect Yourself

Alas, the sad truth is that love doesn't always last forever. These days half of all marriages end in divorce. If you routinely follow the simple (but powerful) advice in the previous section, you'll be in good shape. The number one key to protecting yourself in a serious relationship, financially speaking, is to be fully aware of the current state of what your household owns and what your household owes. Unfortunately, as much as we hope every reader of this book lives happily ever after, we'd be doing you a disservice if we didn't point out a few additional ways to protect yourself financially in a relationship.

1. **Make sure you have at least one credit card on which you are the primary account holder.** This will enable you to establish (or maintain) a credit history in your name in the event your relationship does come to an end. In **CHAPTER 2** we recommended that you have one main credit card, one backup credit card, and if necessary a third one that is used only for reimbursed work expenses. If you choose the backup card as the one on which you are the primary account holder, be sure to charge on it occasionally and *always* pay off the bill on time and in full to establish your own personal credit history.

2. **Think long and hard about consolidating any of your pre-relationship debt.** We realize this may sound harsh, but there are all too many stories of kindhearted women who have taken on their partners' student loan or credit card debt. If you consolidate your debt with your partner's debt, this action can't be undone. Should your relationship not work out, you could find yourself responsible for a portion of that debt.

3. **Stay connected to the finances in your household.** Even if you don't like doing the financial chores and you let your partner take the lead, we recommend you at least review credit card bills and bank/brokerage statements on a regular basis. You need to keep your financial skills fresh, and the only way to do this is to stay involved in your personal finances.

On a separate but related topic, make sure your beneficiary forms are up to date. It is vital to make sure both you and your partner have updated all your employer-sponsored retirement plans, your IRA, and insurance policies to reflect the person(s) you currently want your money to go to in the event of your death. People often name their beneficiaries when they start a job and then forget to update them when life changes happen. This change is very important because the beneficiaries you and your partner designate on these documents will trump your last will and testament.

A Note on Wills and Related Documents

A will states how you want your assets distributed when you die. It's a good idea for everyone to have a will so that your assets get distributed the way you want them to. However, a will is an absolute *must* if you have children who are minors. The reason is that in your will, you can state who you want to be the guardian of your children should you and/or your partner pass away. If you don't name a guardian in your will, the state decides who cares for your children.

You can prepare a basic "do-it-yourself" will using quality online templates from websites such as *www.legalzoom.com* and *www.nolo.com*. If you would like additional help beyond the do-it-yourself option, an estate lawyer should be able to draw up a straightforward will for less than $1,500. To find a reputable estate lawyer in your area, ask friends or coworkers for a recommendation—or check with your local chamber of commerce or bar association for a referral.

Final Considerations

Here are three important things to consider in the context of marriage:

1. **Consider a prenup.** Yes, we know it's not romantic. A prenup (short for "prenuptial agreement") is a document that summarizes how you will handle your finances both during

your marriage and also in the event that your marriage breaks up. If one or both of you come into the marriage with children from a prior marriage and/or significant assets, this is a step worth considering. In fact, even lasting, loving couples can benefit from this type of agreement if its intent is to spell out how assets and liabilities will be handled in your marriage.

2. **If you are a stay-at-home spouse, make sure your IRA is fully funded.** Unfortunately, the government says that one must earn income in order to contribute to an IRA. However, there is a provision to help ensure stay-at-home spouses have retirement security. If you and your spouse file your taxes jointly, and your working spouse earns at least the total amount you want to contribute to both of your IRAs in a given year, each of you can fund your IRA. For example, if the annual per-person IRA limit for that year is $5,500 and your working spouse earns at least $11,000, each of you can contribute $5,500 to your personal IRA. If you are a stay-at-home spouse, you deserve this financial security.

3. **Prince Charming may not know about money, even if he acts like he does.** If something doesn't make sense to you, be sure to keep asking questions until it does. You deserve to understand exactly what is going on with your household's financial situation, so don't let anyone tell you otherwise. ■

Make Sure Your Heart and Your Money Are in Sync

To be in a successful long-term relationship, you both must reveal yourselves—financially speaking.

Create a mutually agreed-upon game plan for how you will deal with budgeting, spending, bill-paying, saving, and investing decisions. It is also critical to commit to at least an annual financial checkup.

Even if it seems your love will last forever, take the steps to protect yourself. (We hope this won't be the case, but you never know.) If things don't work out, you'll be very glad you did.

CHAPTER 16

Time for Action

This chapter is your call to action. Up to this point, we've focused on the practical tools you need to become financially successful. The magic ingredient that will bring it all together is the desire to put these tools to good use.

Money is a very loaded topic. In many ways, it truly is the last taboo in our society. Turn on a television talk show, read news online, or listen to the radio and you'll observe our national propensity to share, share, and share. It seems like nothing is off limits—our relationships, our sexual proclivities, our deepest darkest secrets. We put it all out there, except for our thoughts on money matters. This is unfortunate because your view on money matters is critical to determining your financial success.

Since feelings and emotions about money are so rarely discussed openly, we'd like to end this book by clearing up some common misconceptions about money. Our hope is to inspire you to venture out on your financial journey feeling empowered. Now that you have read this book, you have acquired the knowledge and the tools to achieve financial success. In this final chapter we want to spark your desire to *act* on that knowledge.

Four Empowering Insights about Money

MONEY INSIGHT #1

MOST PEOPLE DON'T HAVE A CLUE ABOUT MONEY, EVEN IF THEY ACT LIKE THEY DO

As we noted in the introduction, most people really don't know how to manage their finances, even if they act like they do. Personal finance is one of those things you're supposed to figure out as you go along. Unfortunately, you get little guidance and typically have few positive role models. To add insult to injury, our society doesn't encourage people to be honest and open about acknowledging any level of financial ignorance. As a result, a lot of what you see is a defensive façade. The numbers bear this out. If you feel like "everyone else has it all figured out" in terms of finances, we're here to tell you that's not so. While it may appear by their car or clothes that some people have made it, don't forget that as of this writing nearly 70 percent of Americans are living paycheck to paycheck. That means that almost three out of four people are just a payday or two away from financial disaster.

MONEY INSIGHT #2

THINGS AREN'T ALWAYS WHAT THEY SEEM

Amazingly, the aforementioned statistic cuts across a wide array of income spectrums. You'd probably be surprised to know just how many families pulling in six-figure incomes (yes, *six figures*) are living paycheck to paycheck as a result of not understanding the basics of how to manage their personal finances. It doesn't matter how much money you make. If you don't save for the future or if you spend more than you earn, you'll end up in serious financial trouble. Think about that the next time you are in a room full of people. How many of them are living in difficult financial conditions, striving to live life-styles that project images well beyond what they can afford? If they all got financially naked, you'd likely be stunned at what you saw.

MONEY INSIGHT #3

LITERALLY *MILLIONS* OF PEOPLE ARE INTIMIDATED BY MONEY MATTERS

Before you read this book you may have thought that money was complex, wished you didn't have to think about it, felt it stressed you out, or possibly were simply embarrassed to talk about the subject. If any of these feelings resonate with you, we're here to say that you are by no means alone. *Millions* of people feel the same way.

MONEY INSIGHT #4

AFTER READING THIS BOOK, *YOU* NOW KNOW MORE THAN THE VAST MAJORITY OF AMERICANS!

It is our hope that after reading *On My Own Two Feet*, you will have both the knowledge and the desire to break free from external pressures—and to build the financial life that's right for you. If you ever find yourself doubting your financial path, please come back and review *On My Own Two Feet*. This book contains the essential elements to enable you to pave your way to financial success, security, and independence. No matter what your current financial situation, you now have the basic knowledge necessary to dramatically improve your personal finances. A successful financial life is all about making choices—the choices that are right for you. Our hope is that you will now make the decisions that are appropriate for you based on what is in your heart and your soul.

▷ We wish you the best of luck with your finances
so you can go out into the world and achieve your
dreams.

Listed on the following pages are the key action items from each chapter of this book. We recommend you use this list as a roadmap against which you measure your progress on your journey toward creating the financial life you want and deserve. If you are interested in suggested resources for continued learning, please see the last section of **APPENDIX C.** ■

What a Modern Girl Needs to Know about Her Personal Finances

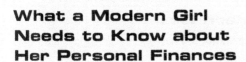

1. Strive to save 15 percent of your gross income.

2. Understand that if you charge something on your credit card and make only the minimum monthly payment, you are effectively paying *twice as much* for that item.

3. Know and protect your credit score; its reach in your life is far and wide.

4. Guard against the unknown with an appropriate amount of insurance for your particular circumstances—health care, auto, and homeowner's insurance (if you own a car/home) are an absolute must. If you have children, life insurance is also essential.

5. Keep in mind your Power Trio of Budgeting guidelines. It's your spending, as opposed to your income, that you have the most control over on a day-to-day basis.

6. Know that you invest for two reasons: to keep the corrosive power of inflation at bay *and* to grow your money faster than inflation.

7. Remember to keep the money you must spend in the next one to five years in a savings account, money market account/fund, or CD. If you are under the age of 50, stocks are where the action is for money you will not need for five or more years.

continued

What a Modern Girl Needs to Know . . . continued

8. When it comes to buying stocks, think index funds—and if you want to keep your financial life really simple, think the S&P 500 index fund.

9. Super-size your retirement nest egg with tax-advantaged accounts.

10. If you need some help prioritizing your savings goals versus your debt repayment, review **CHAPTER 10**.

11. Strive to keep your total monthly housing-related payments to 25 percent or *less* of your monthly gross income.

12. Strive to keep your total monthly car-related payments to 10 percent or *less* of your monthly gross income.

13. Income taxes take a big bite out of your paycheck, so you might as well understand the basics of taxes to ensure no surprises on Tax Day (April 15).

14. Don't let finances ruin your relationship—and don't let your relationship ruin your finances. Reveal yourself, financially speaking, and commit to annual mutual financial checkups.

15. Being financially savvy isn't magic and doesn't take an MBA. You now have the knowledge to create a secure financial future for yourself. It's time to go forth and create the financial life you've always dreamed of!

The Tools for Financial Empowerment

WHERE DOES SAVING 10 PERCENT OF MY GROSS INCOME FOR RETIREMENT GET ME?

The following chart shows approximately where you'll end up in your golden years if you routinely save 10 percent of your gross income every year. The point of this chart is to help you figure out how much your nest egg would enable you to spend per year in your retirement without running out of money.

To read this chart, look down the left column to see the age at which you start your annual savings program and across the top row to find your approximate income level. To calculate how much money you can safely spend each year in retirement, multiply the figure in the chart that corresponds to your age and income level by 5 percent. If you spend no more than 5 percent of your money each year in retirement, you'll have reasonable odds of not outliving your savings over a thirty-year period.

▷ Saving early has a *huge* impact on how comfortable your golden years will be, financially speaking.

Estimate of What You'll Have in Your Retirement Nest Egg by Age 65*

IF YOU ROUTINELY SAVE 10 PERCENT OF YOUR GROSS INCOME EVERY YEAR

Your Age					Your Annual Income Today				
	$20,000	$30,000	$40,000	$50,000	$60,000	$70,000	$80,000	$90,000	$100,000
20	$1,438,000	$2,157,000	$2,876,000	$3,595,000	$4,313,000	$5,032,000	$5,751,000	$6,470,000	$7,189,000
25	$885,000	$1,328,000	$1,770,000	$2,213,000	$2,656,000	$3,098,000	$3,541,000	$3,983,000	$4,426,000
30	$542,000	$813,000	$1,084,000	$1,355,000	$1,626,000	$1,897,000	$2,168,000	$2,439,000	$2,710,000
35	$329,000	$493,000	$658,000	$822,000	$987,000	$1,151,000	$1,316,000	$1,480,000	$1,645,000
40	$197,000	$295,000	$393,000	$492,000	$590,000	$688,000	$787,000	$885,000	$983,000
45	$115,000	$172,000	$229,000	$286,000	$344,000	$401,000	$458,000	$515,000	$573,000
50	$64,000	$95,000	$127,000	$159,000	$191,000	$222,000	$254,000	$286,000	$318,000

*Assumes that you save 10 percent of your gross income a year and that your investments grow 10 percent a year—in line with the long-run return on stocks—with annual salary increases offset by annual inflation. All figures rounded to the nearest $1,000. Note: If savings are invested in a more diversified mix of stocks and bonds (recommended as you get older) expected returns would be lower.

- For example, if you make $50,000 a year and start saving 10 percent of your salary at *age 30*, you'd have the equivalent of $1,355,000 in your nest egg by age 65. With that amount of savings, you'd have over *$67,000 a year* to live on in retirement ($1,355,000 × 0.05 = $67,750).

- If you wait until *age 40* to start saving, you'll only have $492,000 in your nest egg at age 65. That would support annual retirement spending of approximately *$25,000 a year* ($492,000 × 0.05 = $24,600).

- If you wait until *age 50* to start saving, you'll have even less— just $159,000 in your nest egg at age 65. With that amount of savings, you'd have less than *$8,000* a year to live on in retirement ($159,000 × 0.05 = $7,640).

If Social Security is still around, you may get a little something extra from that. However, as of this writing the average female beneficiary receives $1,072 a month from Social Security, so don't expect a windfall.

FROM CHAPTER 1

HOW DO I FIND THE RIGHT BANK FOR DAY-TO-DAY NEEDS?

Here is a list of questions that you can use to find the bank that's right for you:

- Is the bank FDIC insured? If it is, the Federal Depository Insurance Company will insure your bank account up to $250,000 should something bad happen to the bank. *You only want to bank at an FDIC-insured bank.* (You can check your bank's status by going online to *www.fdic.gov* and searching on "Is my bank insured?")

- Does the bank offer free online banking?
- For your checking account, how many checks a month can be written before incurring fees? Is there a minimum account size for checking accounts or any monthly fees?
- Are there ATM withdrawal charges? You should be able to use your bank's ATMs without paying a fee. You'll also want to make sure the bank has ATMs conveniently located near your home and/or office.
- What is the rate of interest offered on savings accounts? Is there a minimum account balance or any monthly fees?

FROM CHAPTER 1

CONTACT INFORMATION FOR FOUR LARGE, ESTABLISHED DISCOUNT BROKERAGE FIRMS

Four large, high-quality, low-cost financial institutions in the United States that we like are Charles Schwab, Fidelity, TIAA-CREF, and Vanguard. These firms typically have lower minimum account sizes than their "traditional brokerage house" cousins. Three newer firms we like are Betterment, Bicycle Financial, and LearnVest. Following is the contact information for these firms.

Firm	Website	Phone Number
Charles Schwab	*www.schwab.com*	866-855-9102
Fidelity	*www.fidelity.com*	800-343-3548
TIAA-CREF	*www.tiaa-cref.org*	800-842-2252
Vanguard	*www.vanguard.com*	877-662-7447

Firm	Website	Phone Number
Betterment	*www.betterment.com*	888-428-9482
LearnVest	*www.learnvest.com*	866-413-7883
Bicycle Financial	*www.bicyclefinancial.com*	(run by Sharon's husband)

FROM CHAPTER 4

RESEARCHING AND COMPARING INSURANCE POLICIES ONLINE

The following websites can be useful in different categories, as the following table outlines, as you shop for various kinds of insurance.

	Health	Auto	Home/ Renter's	Term Life	Disability	Umbrella
www.ehealthinsurance.com	X	—	—	X	X	—
www.insurancefinder.com	X	X	X	X	X	—
www.insurance.com	X	X	X	X	—	—
www.insure.com	X	X	X	X	X	—
www.insweb.com	X	X	X	X	—	—
www.term4sale.com	—	—	—	X	—	—

FROM CHAPTER 5

"POWER TRIO OF BUDGETING" TARGETS IN ACTUAL DOLLARS

The chart on the following page shows, for different salary levels, what you can afford to spend in the different Power Trio of Budgeting categories. These target percentages are rough guides, not absolute recommendations, for your spending. The main goal with these percentages is to make sure that your spending plan provides enough flexibility to let you enjoy today while also prudently planning for tomorrow.

Your Power Trio of Budgeting Targets*

Your YEARLY Gross Income 100%	Your MONTHLY Gross Income 100%	*Minus* Your MONTHLY Income Taxes 25%	Your MONTHLY "Power Trio of Budgeting" 75% (what you have left after taxes)	Your MONTHLY Foundation Expenses 45%	Your MONTHLY Fun Expenses 15%	Your MONTHLY Future Expenses 15% (your savings)
$20,000	$1,670	($420)	$1,250	$750	$250	$250
$25,000	$2,080	($520)	$1,560	$940	$310	$310
$30,000	$2,500	($610)	$1,890	$1,130	$380	$380
$35,000	$2,920	($720)	$2,200	$1,320	$440	$440
$40,000	$3,330	($830)	$2,500	$1,500	$500	$500
$45,000	$3,750	($940)	$2,810	$1,690	$560	$560
$50,000	$4,170	($1,020)	$3,150	$1,890	$630	$630
$55,000	$4,580	($1,130)	$3,450	$2,070	$690	$690
$60,000	$5,000	($1,250)	$3,750	$2,250	$750	$750
$65,000	$5,420	($1,370)	$4,050	$2,430	$810	$810
$70,000	$5,830	($1,430)	$4,400	$2,640	$880	$880
$75,000	$6,250	($1,550)	$4,700	$2,820	$940	$940
$80,000	$6,670	($1,670)	$5,000	$3,000	$1,000	$1,000
$85,000	$7,080	($1,780)	$5,300	$3,180	$1,060	$1,060
$90,000	$7,500	($1,850)	$5,650	$3,390	$1,130	$1,130
$95,000	$7,920	($1,970)	$5,950	$3,570	$1,190	$1,190
$100,000	$8,330	($2,080)	$6,250	$3,750	$1,250	$1,250

*Figures rounded to nearest $10.

FROM CHAPTER 5

TAKING BUDGETING TO THE NEXT LEVEL

The way to take your budgeting to the next level is to look at your two-month spending inventory and use it to set a formal budget. You'll start by identifying the target amount that you plan to spend each month in various categories. You will then track your spending in each category monthly, and as the year progresses you'll compare your actual results to your target results to see if you need to make any adjustments. On the following page is a sample worksheet that you can use if you'd like to take your budgeting process up to this next level. The months between January and December are not shown, but you should fill those in on your worksheet.

		Projected Monthly	Projected Annual	Actual January		Actual December	Actual Average Per Month	Actual Total Per Year
	Sample Budget							
Total Income	**Total Income**							
	Monthly wages or salary (before-tax)							
	Other income (dividends, interest, alimony, etc.)							
	TOTAL GROSS INCOME							
Total Taxes	**Income Taxes**							
	Federal income tax							
	Social Security tax							
	Medicare tax							
	State and local income tax							
	TOTAL INCOME TAXES							
	AFTER-TAX INCOME (Total Gross Income − Total Income Taxes)							
Foundation Expenses	**Housing**							
	Mortgage or rent							
	Property tax							
	Insurance (homeowner's, renter's, umbrella)							
	Utilities (gas, electric, water, phone, cable, Internet)							
	Maintenance and upkeep							
	TOTAL HOUSING EXPENSES							
	Transportation							
	Car payment							
	Car insurance							
	Gas							
	Parking							
	Miscellaneous (AAA, car washes, oil changes)							
	Public transportation							
	TOTAL TRANSPORTA-TION EXPENSES							
	Basic Household Needs							
	Groceries							
	Toiletries and household supplies							
	TOTAL BASIC GROCER-IES AND SUPPLIES							

		Projected Monthly	Projected Annual	Actual January		Actual December	Actual Average Per Month	Actual Total Per Year
	Sample Budget							
Foundation Expenses	**Debt Repayment**							
	Student loans							
	Credit card or other debt repayment							
	TOTAL DEBT PAY DOWN							
	Other Foundation							
	Insurance (medical, life, disability)							
	"Essential" clothing, dry cleaning, alterations, etc.							
	Child-care expenses							
	Charitable giving							
	Other foundation expenses							
	TOTAL OTHER FOUNDATION							
	TOTAL FOUNDATION EXPENSES							
Fun Expenses	**Fun Food**							
	Take-out							
	Coffees and snacks							
	Restaurant meals or drinks							
	TOTAL FUN FOOD							
	Entertainment							
	Movies, music, concerts							
	Books, magazines, newspapers							
	Hobbies							
	Other entertainment							
	TOTAL ENTERTAINMENT							
	Other Items							
	Personal care							
	"Want" clothing and accessories							
	Vacations							
	Gifts							
	Pets							
	Miscellaneous							
	TOTAL OTHER ITEMS							
	TOTAL FUN EXPENSES							
	TOTAL SAVED for FUTURE EXPENSES (After-Tax Income minus Foundation and Fun Expenses)							

The Path from Saving to Investing

A YEAR-BY-YEAR LOOK AT STOCK MARKET RETURNS

The table on the facing page shows the year-by-year returns for the S&P 500 from 1926 to 2012. As you look at this table, the main thing to focus on is the colors. The green boxes show the years when the stock market went up, while the black boxes show the years when the market was either flat or went down.

It's interesting to note that while stocks generated an average per-year return of around 10 percent during the nearly ninety years from 1926 to 2012, those returns have been very lumpy:

- In twenty-two of those years, stocks actually *lost* money.
- In fourteen of those years, stocks generated investment returns that were positive, but *less* than 10 percent per year.
- In fifty-one of those years, stocks generated investment returns greater than 10 percent per year.

As you can see from this table, while stocks have gone up nicely over time, there have been individual years when the going got rough. Looking at investment returns over every historical five-year period from 1926 to 2012 (for example, 1926–1931, 1927–1932, 1928–1933, and so on) provides interesting insight into history. You'll see that in over 85 percent of historical five-year time periods, stocks generated positive investment returns. That also means in nearly 15 percent of historical five-year time periods, stocks generated negative investment returns. However, if you stretch out the period to ten years, you'll see that in over 95 percent of these historical time periods, stocks generated positive investment returns. This is precisely why you should not put money in stocks that you can't afford to leave there for at least five, and ideally at least ten, years.

Year	Total Return	Year	Total Return	Year	Total Return
1926	11.6%	1952	18.4%	1978	6.6%
1927	37.5%	1953	-0.1%	1979	18.4%
1928	43.6%	1954	52.6%	1980	32.4%
1929	-8.4%	1955	31.6%	1981	-4.9%
1930	-24.9%	1956	6.6%	1982	21.4%
1931	-43.3%	1957	-10.8%	1983	22.5%
1932	-8.2%	1958	43.4%	1984	6.3%
1933	54.0%	1959	12.0%	1985	32.2%
1934	-1.4%	1960	0.5%	1986	18.5%
1935	47.7%	1961	26.9%	1987	5.2%
1936	33.9%	1962	-8.7%	1988	16.8%
1937	-35.0%	1963	22.8%	1989	31.5%
1938	31.1%	1964	16.5%	1990	-3.1%
1939	-0.1%	1965	12.5%	1991	30.6%
1940	-0.1%	1966	-10.1%	1992	7.7%
1941	-11.6%	1967	24.0%	1993	10.0%
1942	20.3%	1968	11.1%	1994	1.3%
1943	25.9%	1969	-8.5%	1995	37.4%
1944	19.8%	1970	4.0%	1996	23.1%
1945	36.4%	1971	14.3%	1997	33.4%
1946	-8.1%	1972	19.0%	1998	28.6%
1947	5.7%	1973	-14.7%	1999	21.0%
1948	5.5%	1974	26.5%	2000	-9.1%
1949	18.8%	1975	37.2%	2001	-11.9%
1950	31.7%	1976	23.8%	2002	-22.1%
1951	24.0%	1977	-7.2%	2003	27.9%

chart continues

Year	Total Return
2004	10.6%
2005	4.7%
2006	15.7%

Year	Total Return
2007	5.5%
2008	-37.0%
2009	26.5%

Year	Total Return
2010	15.1%
2011	2.1%
2012	16.0%

FROM CHAPTERS 7 AND 8

HOW TO BUY INDEX FUNDS AT THE BIG DISCOUNT BROKERAGE FIRMS

In Chapters 7 and 8, we referenced several different index funds. Listed below are the official names of these funds at each of the discount brokerage firms mentioned in **APPENDIX A**. The letters you see in the parentheses are called ticker symbols. A ticker symbol is simply a shorthand way of identifying a mutual fund or a stock. Each discount brokerage firm has its own minimum account size, but know that they will often drop this figure if you commit to making automatic regular monthly deposits. Be sure to ask a customer service representative about this exception to the minimum account size, as they may forget to discuss this option.

	"S&P 500" Index Fund (large U.S.-based companies)	"Extended Market" Index Fund (small and medium-sized U.S.-based companies)	"International" Index Fund (large companies based outside the U.S.)
Vanguard	Vanguard 500 Index Fund Investor Shares (VFINX)	Vanguard Extended Market Index Fund Investor Shares (VEXMX)	Vanguard Emerging Markets Stock Index Fund (VEIEX)
Fidelity	Spartan 500 Index Fund Investor Class (FSMKX)	Spartan Extended Market Index Investor Class (FSEMX)	Spartan Emerging Markets Index Fund Investor Class (FPEMX)

Charles Schwab	Schwab S&P 500 Index Fund Investor Shares (SWPIX)	Schwab Small Cap Index Fund Investor Shares (SWSMX)	Schwab International Index Fund (SWIXX)

Recall that in **APPENDIX A**, we listed contact information for each of these three firms.

FROM CHAPTER 8

TWO CLASSIC INVESTMENT PITFALLS TO AVOID WHEN BUYING ACTIVELY MANAGED MUTUAL FUNDS OR INDIVIDUAL STOCKS

When it comes to investing, most people try to find the next hot stock. Ironically, studies show that over the long run, the ability to avoid key pitfalls has a lot more influence on investment success than the attempt to hit home runs. Below we discuss the two classic investment pitfalls to avoid.

Pitfall #1: Not Understanding the Math Behind Losing Money

At a dinner party, Helen overheard someone talking about how he had bought shares in CoolCo and doubled his money in two months. So she bought shares of CoolCo. Instead of going up, however, Helen's shares in CoolCo declined in value by 50 percent during her first month.

Guess how much Helen's investment would have to increase just to *break even* on her original investment? Most people would say up 50 percent. But the answer is actually up 100 percent. Here's the math:

- Helen started with $1,000 but it dropped to $500.
- In order for her $500 to get back to $1,000 it has to double (meaning it has to go up 100 percent).

Unfortunately, the numbers get worse the deeper the initial decline. For instance, if you have a stock that drops 80 percent, it has to go up a whopping 400 percent just to *break even*. It may not sound exciting to pursue the long-run returns of an index fund. However, it's a tried-and-true strategy—a classic example of the tortoise beating the hare.

Pitfall #2: Getting Nervous and Not Holding On for the Long Term

Harriet wants to be financially empowered. However, when she checks her investments and sees they have declined, it makes her feel seasick. So when Harriet's stocks go down, she sells them. Then she waits for them to go back up before buying them again. Harriet is proud of herself. She thinks she's being very prudent.

There is a strong human tendency to want to buy a stock while it is going up and to dump it at the first sign of trouble. This tendency results in panic, in which investors end up buying high and selling low. That's the exact opposite of what you need to do to make money.

Eye-opening data from Dimensional Fund Advisors shows that Harriet is not alone:

- An investor who bought an S&P 500 index fund in 1970 and held onto it through thick and thin until the end of 2012 would have generated an average investment gain of *9.9 percent* per year over those forty-two years or 10,750 trading days (despite the fact that in a number of those years the S&P 500 index fund *lost* money).

- However if you got ants in your financial pants and tried to jump in and out of the market and missed just the best twenty-five trading days (out of 10,750 days) your return would be cut by a whopping third. You'd have earned just 6.3 percent.

- To put some dollar signs around that, $1,000 invested in 1970 and left alone until the end of the year in 2012 would have been worth $58,769. But if you missed just twenty-five of the best days over that forty-two-year stretch that $1,000 would have grown to just $13,999. Now that's a steep price to pay for trying to "time" the market.

FROM CHAPTER 8

IF YOU WANT TO LEARN MORE ABOUT INVESTING

If you're interested in learning more about investing, we recommend the following books:

- *The Random Walk Guide to Investing: Ten Rules for Financial Success*, by Burton G. Malkiel. If you want to read just one other book on investing, this is the one we recommend. This book is a concise, straightforward primer on investing written by a world-renowned Princeton University economics professor.

- *The Little Book of Common Sense Investing*, by John Bogle. Another must-read for any serious student of investing. With his trademark straightforward prose, Vanguard founder John Bogle tells you what to pay attention to—and what to ignore—when it comes to growing your wealth with discipline.

● *Investing Made Simple*, by Michael Piper. This slim book packs a powerful punch. A few hours snuggled up with this book and you will find your understanding of and confidence in the long-run process of investing has soared.

FROM CHAPTER 9

WHAT TO DO IF YOUR EMPLOYER-SPONSORED RETIREMENT SAVINGS PLAN DOESN'T OFFER INDEX FUNDS

The unfortunate reality is that many employer-sponsored retirement savings plans do not offer index funds. If this is your employer's situation, ask your plan administrator to help you identify the actively managed mutual fund that most closely resembles the index fund you prefer. For instance, if you are hoping to get an actively managed fund that is closest to the S&P 500 index, you'll want to make sure the fund is focused on large U.S.-based companies. You'll also want to ask for an actively managed mutual fund that has high-quality diversified holdings with low turnover and a low expense ratio. "Low turnover" simply means that the fund manager isn't doing a lot of buying and selling of stocks in the fund.

If you can't invest in an index fund (or an actively managed fund that closely resembles an index fund) a target-date retirement fund is a solid alternative.

A target-date retirement fund is a pool of money that shifts its weightings among stocks, bonds, and cash as you get closer to retirement. You decide the year in which you think you will retire and then select a fund with the date (or range of dates) closest to that year. These funds tend to have names like "Target Fund 2040" or "Target Retirement 2050." For instance, if you are 35 years old in 2013 and you think you'll retire in thirty years, you'd choose a target fund with a date of 2045.

FROM CHAPTER 9

HOW TO MOVE MONEY FROM YOUR FORMER EMPLOYER'S RETIREMENT SAVINGS PLAN INTO A ROLLOVER IRA

- **Step #1:** Open up a rollover IRA account at the same discount brokerage firm where you have your Roth or traditional IRA.
- **Step #2:** Ask the human resources or benefits department at your former employer for the forms needed to send the money in your employer-sponsored retirement savings plan directly to the rollover IRA account you just opened up.
- **Step #3:** Make sure that your employer-sponsored retirement savings plan gets transferred *directly* from your former employer to your rollover IRA account. Under no circumstances do you want the check made out to you, as that will trigger all sorts of financial headaches.

FROM CHAPTER 10

HOW BEST TO SAVE FOR YOUR CHILDREN'S COLLEGE EDUCATION

There are two main types of tax-advantaged accounts that can help you save for your children's college education:

- **529 plan:** A 529 plan is a special tax-exempt account to which you can contribute after-tax money for your children's education. It is tax-advantaged because investment gains are not taxed if used for qualified educational expenses. The 529 plans are run by individual states, so your investment options are limited to a pre-selected group of mutual funds decided on by each state. The good news is that you don't have to invest in your own state's plan (though if you do, you may get a state tax benefit). As of this writing our three favorite state plans in alphabetical order are Alaska, Nevada, and Utah.

- **Coverdell Educational Savings Account (ESA):** This is another special tax-exempt account to which you can contribute after-tax money for educational expenses. As with a Roth IRA, there are income limits to qualify for opening this type of account. At the time of this writing, your income needs to be less than $110,000 if you are single or less than $220,000 if you are married to contribute to this type of account. If you qualify, you can put $2,000 a year as of this writing into this account until your child is 18 years old. You can open this type of account at your discount brokerage firm and invest it in the index fund(s) of your choice.

Which account is right for you? Unfortunately, this is a complex topic, and there is not a one-size-fits-all answer. If you want to learn more about these two plans and saving for college in general, we recommend you do additional research online, at *www.savingfor college.com.*

APPENDIX C

The Strategies for Real-Life Situations

THE MOST COMMON TAX FORMS

What forms will you need to do your tax return? For the vast majority of people, tax filing requirements will be met with just a few key forms.

▷ The form that all taxpayers must fill out is Form 1040.

Form 1040, the basic tax return, comes in several versions. The 1040 EZ is the short, easy version. The 1040A is a little more detailed, but it gives you more opportunities to reduce your tax bill. Finally, the 1040 is the version you'll use if you are going to itemize your deductions. There are additional forms you may need based on your specific tax situation, as follows.

Tax Form	Purpose
Schedule A	To itemize your deductions
Schedule B	For any interest and/or dividend income
Schedule C	If you are self-employed, for listing your revenues and expenses*

Schedule D	For gains or losses from the sales of stocks, bonds, or other investments
Form 4868	If you can't get your taxes done by April 15 and need to file for an extension. Note, even if you file an extension, you must still pay any tax owed by April 15.

*If your self-employment income is $400 or more, you must pay Social Security and Medicare taxes on those earnings and also fill out Schedule SE.

These days you can file your taxes with the IRS electronically, as opposed to mailing them in. The IRS claims that people make fewer mistakes when they file electronically, and they receive any refund due much faster. If you are doing your own taxes, you can get more details on this at *www.irs.gov.*

FROM CHAPTER 16

SUGGESTED ADDITIONAL WEB RESOURCES AND READING
In the introduction to this book we quoted John Naisbitt, who said that our society is "Drowning in information and starved for knowledge." The goal of *On My Own Two Feet* is to address this conundrum by providing you with one-stop shopping for the basics of personal finance. If you wish to delve deeper into any of the topics we've discussed, following is a list of recommended personal finance websites and books.

Suggested Web Resources

- *www.bicyclefinancial.com*: Answer seven simple questions and get custom-tailored financial advice in a box to help you address those vital daily financial questions that can seem so overwhelming. Whether it's figuring out what debt to pay down first or whether to allocate savings to a 401(k) or an IRA, this innovative firm will help you find the answer in a snap.

- *www.findabetterbank.com* and *www.culookup.com*: If you are shopping for a new place for your day-to-day cash.

- *www.gogirlfinance.com*, *www.dailyworth.com*, *www.learnvest.com*: Three wonderful sites for women, each with a daily newsletter you can sign up for to receive financial wisdom right in your inbox. We love all three.

- *www.savvyladies.com*: Nonprofit founded by Stacy Francis with thousands of women around the country coming together on webinars and through their monthly newsletter to self-empower around personal finance.

- *www.mymoney.gov*: Run by the U.S. Financial Literacy and Education Commission, this website provides a treasure trove of information on personal finance.

Suggested Books

- *Get Financially Naked: How to Talk Money with Your Honey*, by Manisha Thakor and Sharon Kedar. Millions of couples struggle with financial tensions in their household. You do not have to be one of them. This book will give you clear, simple, practical tools you can use to make sure money does not come between you and your mate.

- *Overcoming Underearning*, by Barbara Stanny. Written by the iconic and groundbreaking woman and money chronicler, this book helps you overcome the self-imposed condition of underearning (living paycheck to paycheck, struggling with debt, and tolerating low pay). Read this time-tested classic book and you will not only learn five essential steps to financial independence, you'll also feel empowered and confident in your value.

- *Pay It Down!*, by Jean Chatzky. If you are struggling with the burden of credit card or other debt, this book explains how you can "go from debt to wealth on $10 a day." We highly recommend this book if you are working on paying down your debt.

- *The Total Money Makeover*, by Dave Ramsey. Written by the founder of "Financial Peace University," this book gives you personal finance tough love like no other. It's an essential guidebook for anyone who feels like they've taken a financial wrong turn and is committed to a fresh start.

- *Women's Worth*, by Eleanor Blayney, CFP®. Founder of Direction for Women and CFP Board Consumer Advocate Eleanor Blayney has written a classic guide on women and money. Her frank approach intersperses practical advice with easy-to-do exercises that will help you understand your beliefs about money, learn the fundamentals of financial planning, and gain confidence in your financial know-how. This book belongs on every woman's bookshelf.

- *Your Money or Your Life,* by Joe Dominguez and Vicki Robin. If you want to simplify your life and refocus on what really, truly matters for you, this book is just what the doctor ordered. Both of the authors left high-powered jobs to focus on the things in life that really made them happy. In this book they explain how you can do the same.

Acknowledgments

As many writers before us have noted, a book is never a solitary project. We thank our families for their love and support. This book would not be possible without them. We also thank our terrific team of professionals who turned our idea into a reality: our agent Bill Gladstone of Waterside Productions, PR and media maven Meryl L. Moss, the entire team at Adams Media, and an extra big thank you to Shalon Ironroad, whose tireless research made the submission of this second updated edition "on time, and in full" possible.

About the Authors

Manisha Thakor is the founder/CEO of MoneyZen Wealth Management, where she and her team provide holistic, joy-based financial life planning and investment management services for women and families with $1 million to $25+ million in investible assets. Manisha is also an ardent financial literacy advocate for women of all income and wealth levels, serving as a Financial Fellow at Wellesley College, sitting on the national board of the Girl Scouts of the USA, and through her writings as a *Wall Street Journal* expert panelist and other media. Manisha earned an MBA from Harvard Business School, a BA from Wellesley College, and is a CFA charterholder. She lives in Santa Fe, New Mexico, with her husband. Manisha's website is *www.moneyzen.com*.

Sharon Kedar is a business executive, mother, and advocate for practical feminism. She is a managing director at a top-tier global investment management firm. Sharon earned her MBA from Harvard Business School and is a CFA charterholder. Sharon's financial literacy advocacy work has been featured in a wide range of national media including *BusinessWeek*, *U.S. News & World Report*, the *Huffington Post*, *NBC Nightly News*, and *Oprah & Friends Radio*. Sharon's website is *www.sharonkedar.com*.

INDEX